I WENT THROUGH THIS FOR YOU

Lauren Freeman

Sylvia Black

Renee Blair

Nakeisha Freeman

Chas Dixon

Monique Sharp

Kristina Lizhnyak

ISBN: 978-1-970179-35-4

FIRST EDITION

For more information, please visit: www.throughthisforyou.com
Book Project Management: Raindrop Creative Inc/StartWrite Division
Editors: Lauren Freeman & Tiara Brown | http://raindropbrand.com
Cover Direction/Design: Donovan Purvey | http://dkgrafx.com

Scripture Reference:

Table of Contents

"When Pain Becomes Purpose"

All my life, I have known I was going to do something *amazing*. I want to be clear—not amazing as the world defines it, not fame or applause. I mean, amazing as only God designs. The kind that starts quietly in your heart and doesn't let go until you act.

This book is what I was meant to create. Its purpose is to turn personal pain into meaningful purpose, offering connection and hope to others.

I grew up surrounded predominantly by women. My family was a collective of feminine energy—stories shared around tables, in kitchens, in living rooms, in the kind of honest conversation that women have when they trust each other. And because of that environment, I became a person who genuinely thrives in the presence of other women. I have never been someone who struggles to empathize with another woman's experience. I have never carried ill will toward feminine energy. If anything, I have always been drawn toward it—curious about it, moved by it, protective of it. I believe my upbringing was God-ordained. He was preparing me, long before I understood what I was being prepared for.

I am also a writer by nature. An English teacher. A lover of books and stories—biographies, autobiographies, narratives that take you through the full arc of someone's life. Something happens to me when I read a well-told story. Something that feels almost sacred. To sit inside someone else's experience, to feel what they felt, to understand what they understood—that kind of empathy is extraordinary to me. And I have always known, somewhere deep and certain, that one day I would write something.

* * *

In middle school, I found The Joy Luck Club in the library. It's a story of Chinese-American women—mothers and daughters—passing pain and unspoken wounds from one generation to the next. The mothers didn't always know; the daughters didn't always perceive. But these quiet transfers shaped their lives. The book journeys through how, what, and why this happens. I was mesmerized.

I later discovered it had been made into a movie, and of course, I watched it. But that was also my first real encounter with the truth that a novel—a narrative—takes you into places a film simply cannot reach. The book is always better than the movie, and that was the moment I understood why. A story on a page invites you in. It doesn't show you someone's face and tell you what to feel. It hands you the words and lets you feel it for yourself. That book planted something in me that never went away.

Years later, I watched the movie Enough. In one scene, Jennifer Lopez is in a car with her daughter after escaping her abusive husband. Deciding to leave, she says she always knew there would come a point when she would absorb pain for her daughter—suffering in advance so her daughter wouldn't have to. That line changed me.

Together, the lessons from The Joy Luck Club and the pivotal moment in Enough form the foundation of this book. *I Went*

Through This for You means that the pain we experienced was not wasted. Seven women have shared their stories here, so your path might feel lighter, strengthened by what we've learned.

* * *

I have known this book was coming for at least ten years.

I knew its name and purpose. But I didn't know who would be in it—some hadn't entered my life yet. God had a sequence. I carried on knowing and waited.

When the time came, I approached seven women. I chose them specifically because of the breadth of their stories—the diaspora of experience that each one of them represents. Some of them I have known for years. Some I had known for less than twelve months when God placed them on my heart for this project. Some are family. Some are friends I have walked through life beside, women whose stories I have witnessed up close, whose tears I have sat with, and whose rebuilding I have cheered.

Every single one of them said yes.

I knew they would say yes—I know their hearts and what we care about: the woman on the other side. The one who picks up this book in desperation, grief, confusion, or the deep loneliness of feeling unseen. We built this for her. I am one of these seven women. My story lives in these pages too—in Chapter Two and again in Chapter Ten. But before you get there, I need you to understand why I built this. Because I have known for ten years that this book existed. I spent that time waiting for the women, waiting for the moment, waiting for God to say now. And when He did, everything came together in a way that could only be described as designed.

* * *

Here is how this book is structured, so you know what you are walking into: Part One is called The Breaking. In it, you will meet each of these seven women at a defining moment—the history they carried, the turning points that changed everything, the places where life did not go the way they planned, hoped, or prayed. Each chapter ends in a cliffhanger because that is how cliffhangers feel in real time. You don't get a resolution at the moment. You only get the weight of what just happened.

Chapter Nine sits in the middle. It is a pause—a pivot point—before you enter the second half of the book. It exists to shift your perspective before the stories continue. We will talk there about why any of this happens at all. Why does God allow what He allows? What it means when the thing you survived turns out to be bigger than just you.

Part Two is called The Rebuilding. The same seven women. The same stories. But now you see what God did next. Now you see the aftermath, the healing, the surrender, the second chances, the second loves, and the second callings. Now you see what happens when a woman refuses to let her pain be the last word.

The final chapter speaks to you. By then, you'll know you are the eighth woman. Your story belongs here—even if your name isn't on the cover. One day, what you survived will be what someone else needs.

* * *

To the woman holding this book: I know it is hard. I know that at times it does not make sense. I know what it feels like to carry something heavy and look around and wonder why no one else seems to see the weight of it. I know what it feels like to survive something and still not quite understand why it happened to you. We, seven women, know too.

This book is our hand reaching back. Our hearts, broken and offered to you, so you don't feel alone in your burden. We see you. We know why you picked this up. Before you read a story, know it was built for you.

There is something here for you—from disappointment to heartbreak, loss to redemption, loneliness that hollows, and love that rebuilds. You'll find yourself in these stories. Maybe in one. Maybe all. Overall, you'll finish feeling seen.

Get ready for a journey of tears—but also something steadier. Permission. Permission to keep going, to know your pain was not wasted, to reach back for someone standing where you once stood. That is the point.

We went through this for *you*.

PART I
The Breaking

Seven women. Seven stories.

Chapter 1

Lauren's Story

———◆———

"Searching for Love in All the Wrong Places"

My early childhood is a blur. Not because anything particularly dramatic happened in those first years, but because they lacked any real sense of anything. My mom and dad were high school sweethearts who got married when my mom was almost nine months pregnant. Eventually, it didn't work out. They both moved on, maintaining a seemingly decent friendship. My mom remarried, and life felt pretty normal. That is, until it wasn't.

* * *

I don't remember arriving at the courthouse. I don't remember a conversation explaining where I was going or why. What I remember is being placed in a room   toys, snacks, parents sitting at a careful distance. It was quiet in the way adults make spaces quiet when something serious is happening, and they don't want the children to fully understand it yet.

I remember meeting another young girl there. I looked at her and thought: I know why I'm here. But why are you here? To my surprise, it was the same reason. She was there to testify against someone who had done something inappropriate to her. She didn't say exactly what had happened, but something in me could already tell that her story was worse than mine. That whatever had earned her a ticket to this room—with its toys and snacks and quietly watchful adults—was something harder than what I had lived. And if she, someone who seemed smaller and more fragile than I, was brave enough to do this, then I could do it too.

What my young mind could not prepare for was the nature of what testifying actually meant. I now understand what it means to take a stand and speak the truth. But the courtroom is not a space designed to help the one who was hurt. The questions come from every angle, in different forms, repeated back to you in different framings, each one designed to create doubt about what you know you experienced. The defense attorney was polite in a way that was not authentic—direct, absolute, methodical. She asked me over and over about how the man I had known as a father figure had gained access to the most private part of me.

"Did he pull your panties down or to the side?" she asked.

Then: "So you say to the side? How?"

My stomach dropped; I had told this story thousands of times since the first hours after the event. Yet again: "To the side," I told her.

She pressed—"So you're sure?"—and I broke, shouting out the worst part before burying my face to cry.

She said nothing else.

I learned something in that room that I would carry for a long time without fully naming it. That there is no payment for certain violations. The burden of proving what someone did to you will often leave you more broken than the act itself. That the responsibility of speaking truth on behalf of justice is a weight that no child should have to carry alone. I carried it. And then I moved right on to the next grade, and my brain did what brains do when they are too young to process—it suppressed the whole season and buried it deep.

* * *

The timeline jumped forward again: the summer after fifth grade brought another courtroom. This time it was because of my dad. He had been convicted of money laundering along with other things I didn't fully understand, and he was asking my stepsister and me to write letters on his behalf—letters of sympathy to the judge that might help reduce his sentence. I didn't fully understand the scope of the work I was being asked to do. What I understood was that it mattered to him. That he was going away, and that my letter might shorten how long.

I wrote about how great my dad was and how much I needed him, pouring my heart onto the page and describing needs I didn't yet fully understand. I remember his sentencing. His courtroom felt warmer than mine—wood everywhere, a different light. After the closing argument, the judge announced his sentence. Everyone around me cheered. I felt a dagger in my heart. Standing there, I realized: the same attorney who had cross-examined me as a child—the one who made me shout my worst memory in front of strangers—had also defended my dad. He told me he hired her because she "did a good job." In his way, he helped me see that as a good thing. I hid the pain and moved on, learning to put others' feelings above my pain. Time didn't heal, but it moved things forward. I would rely on that for a long time.

* * *

My dad left that year, and life started a new chapter without him.

I had tested into a magnet program for gifted and talented students—something that should have been a moment of celebration, but arrived wrapped in everything else that was happening. My mom made the sacrifice to get me there. Early mornings, traffic, her time, and energy poured into making it possible. She didn't say much, but I could always tell she was proud. I could feel it in those cold early mornings when she got up and fought through traffic beside me. Her sacrifice was enough.

I excelled because I genuinely wanted to. For the first time, I was surrounded by others who were equally smart—not the only one, but one among many. I finally felt intellectually challenged, and I loved it.

In those classes, I knew what set me apart. Everyone else had a mom and dad, nice houses, siblings—a seemingly complete life. Mine didn't. My dad's absence created a ripple. His wife, grieving, decided quickly to move on. So I did, too. Brief bonding—visits, a sense of togetherness—became exile. I was moved out, distanced from my little brother, my only blood sibling on that side. It all happened fast.

To make things easier on my mom, I mostly stayed with my paternal grandmother. It was just the two of us, and our bond was unlike anything else in my life. She was the steady presence I needed. Still, I longed for my mom. Part of me wanted her to ask me to stay. Now I understand why she let me go—there were lessons I needed from a seasoned woman of faith that she knew she couldn't yet teach. She also carried her own guilt about what had happened to me as a child, guilt that made her afraid to fail me again.

* * *

Several years later, the summer before eighth grade, rumors started circulating that my dad was being released. By then, my life was shifting. I'd already fallen in love—or what I thought was love. And I'd given away my last bit of innocence.

It wasn't a terrible experience, which in some ways made it harder to understand later. In my barely teenage mind, I believed he truly cared for me. We had grown up around each other, so it felt natural—almost inevitable. He was gentle and showed consideration for my feelings, at least as much as a fifteen-year-old boy can. I believed him.

Until six months later, when I learned he would be a teenage father. Not from our one experience, but from several others he had with someone else. That is how I learned that being chosen in a moment is not the same as being chosen.

* * *

Eventually, the time I had been waiting for arrived: my dad came home. The whole family was excited—my grandmother, my aunt, everyone. It was a school day, so I couldn't be there for the pickup, but my anxiety was high for good reasons. I had kept visiting him while he was away, and my experience of him was always good. I was truly excited to have him back.

He came home and hit the ground running. His first mission: get me a car. He taught me to drive, helped me get my license, and bought me one. It all arrived like a rushing wind—the provider version of him, the father-who-shows-up. His sister had a job waiting; everything was in place. During that season, he gave me plenty of attention. He came to my cheerleading events. He was present.

But his version of being present had a quality I didn't have words for then. He played the cool dad—welcoming every guy I ever brought around with open arms, calling them his son-in-law, trusting anyone with me without question. Looking back, I think part of that came from his own history. In his eyes, these boys were probably better than he had been at their age. But what I felt was something different. It felt like he didn't have any standards for me. Like I wasn't worth protecting.

So, the pattern continued. High school meant dating, heartbreak, then repeating the cycle. Each relationship was an attempt to find something I had long been missing—something I could only feel, not name.

* * *

I just knew college would be different. Before that, I had always blamed the boys. They were young. Immature. But I was also afraid to date older men—somewhere inside me, I feared the responsibility that came with adult relationships. Maybe it was the scars from childhood. Maybe it was the quiet voice that had never fully learned to trust. But on my very first day of college, I met someone.

He was handsome, though unaware of it—not exactly my type, if I even had one. What mattered was his consistency and commitment. Somehow, I settled in his presence as I never had before. We navigated college together. We went to class, and sometimes we didn't, but we were together—and no matter what party he went to, I could trust him. He never violated that. Everyone knew we were together, and that meant something to me. For the first time in a long time, I felt safe inside a relationship.

And then one day, he came to me and said things were getting serious, and he thought we should slow down. I heard a breakup.

I was devastated. He wasn't trying to end things—he just wasn't ready to get married the following week—but I couldn't hear the difference. So we broke up, and I moved back home to Fort Worth.

If I'm honest, I had been severely distracted—not just by him but by trying to survive college in another city on financial aid alone. I needed to reset. I went back to my grandmother's, enrolled at UTA, and dove into church the way I always had—fully, completely, as my safe space. I learned so much about God and prayer in that season.

Slowly, Jason and I reconnected. My grandmother warned me. My pastor warned me. He questioned whether our values were truly aligned—I was serious about the Lord, and Jason didn't even go to church at the time. But I felt like his curiosity about faith was enough. I convinced myself that meant we could grow into it together.

Then I found out I was pregnant. I didn't even need a test to confirm it. I just knew. My grandmother came to me shortly after. She asked me one question: Do you want to be married? Then she opened her Bible and showed me the Scriptures. She talked to me about doing things God's way. And I prayed harder than I had ever prayed in my life.

And when I did—Jason showed up. He moved across Texas, and he married me. Because this was exactly what I had asked God for, I took it as His approval. I took it as confirmation. I was twenty-one years old, standing there with a ring on my finger and a baby growing inside of me, and I believed my life had finally fallen into place.

What I didn't understand then—what I couldn't have understood yet—is that sometimes God allows us to receive exactly what we ask for so that we can learn the difference between our will and His. I believed God had answered my prayers. What I didn't know yet was that the lesson He was about to teach me about the difference between the two would change the course of my entire life.

Chapter 2

Sylvia's Story

—◆—

"The Choice That Never Left Me"

I've always wanted to be a mom. Not in a vague, someday way—I had a *real* plan. I'd marry first, then have at least two children. I decided this at nine, with certainty only a child has. Uncomplicated. Unshakeable. Absolutely sure.

Even before I had language for it, I was wired to nurture. In kindergarten, when kids played house, I was always the mom—not because anyone assigned me, but because it was where I naturally landed. I felt drawn to caring for people and encouraging what they didn't always see in themselves. It was less a personality trait than a calling I was born with.

Looking back now, I know that was God. It had to be—because what I was watching at home was not a blueprint for motherhood. Instead, it was a survival story that deeply shaped my understanding of what it means to be a mom.

My mom was doing the best she could as a single parent, and she was doing it hard. I watched her carry things that would have broken most people. She was resourceful and determined and present in the ways she knew how to be. But watching her be a mom was also watching someone navigate life from a place of constant challenge. If you had observed it from the outside, you might have walked away thinking, absolutely not—I am never having children. And I think a lot of people in my position would have come to exactly that conclusion.

Yet, for me, a different pull persisted. Something deeper held me to the vision I had as a child. I believe that's because of what God placed in me before I could choose for myself. That nurturing gift—the urge to help people wherever they are—wasn't shaped by my environment. Therefore, it couldn't be extinguished by it. *The proof is that I always ended up being the mom when we played house.*

Being the oldest daughter shaped me early. In our culture, older siblings help—it's understood. When my mom became a single parent, I stepped in without being asked: doing my sister's hair, making sure she was ready for school, watching over what needed attention. That responsibility felt natural, not burdensome. It was simply who I was.

And underneath all of it was this quiet, steady vision of what I was building toward. A home with a husband and children, a two-parent foundation, the kind of stability I had witnessed in glimpses and believed in completely. That desire never left me. It just had to wait longer than I planned, in ways I could not have predicted, through seasons that would test every single thing I thought I believed about God's faithfulness.

✶ ✶ ✶

Academically, I was what people called a golden child. Straight A's. No behavioral problems. No drama. I never gave my parents reason to worry—except, of course, for the attitudes that come with being the eldest daughter, which any eldest daughter will understand.

Task-oriented from a young age, I always had a plan. College was never a question—it was the natural next step. Inspired by a high school teacher who had been a nurse and transitioned to teaching, I chose nursing early on. She explained the difference between an associate's and a bachelor's degree, and showed me the many possible directions a nursing career could take: working in a hospital, moving into education, specializing, or continuing to grow within the profession.

That was what drew me in—not just security, but possibility. I wanted a respectable profession that would provide long-term stability, one where opportunities would always be available to me. Nursing checked every box. So when I got to undergrad, the mission was to graduate with a nursing degree. Everything else would follow. What I did not plan for was the relationship that would complicate everything.

I was seventeen when I met him—online, back when meeting someone that way was still a relatively new and largely unregulated thing. He was six years older than me, twenty-three, and he was completely upfront about his age and his life from the beginning. He wasn't hiding anything. He knew exactly how old I was and what I was working toward, and instead of being a distraction, he seemed genuinely invested in helping me get there.

He kept my '90 Corolla running for four years. He wrote flashcards, filled my gas tank, and made nursing school manageable. My parents disliked the age gap, but knew I was independent. They let it be, even if reluctantly.

At seventeen, I was in love—utterly convinced it was real and unable to imagine beyond the moment. At that moment, everything was good, and I had more than enough.

* * *

I was deep in finals when I noticed my cycle was four days late. Up until that point, Mother Nature had always been reliable in my life—regular, predictable, never a source of anxiety. Four days were not something I could easily dismiss. But I tried. I told myself it was the stress of finals. I told my boyfriend, and he said exactly what I needed to hear at that moment: it was probably just stress, and if my cycle hadn't come after finals, we would take a test together. He knew the nursing degree was the priority. He knew I had a timeline, and nothing was supposed to derail it. He was trying to protect the plan.

Then I failed anatomy and physiology by four points. *Four points*. I had pulled all-nighters before and came through. I had pushed through exhaustion, stress, and the ordinary difficulties of a demanding program. But this time, four points separated me from the next step in everything I had been working toward. Without passing A&P, I couldn't apply to nursing school. The timeline I had mapped out so precisely was suddenly in pieces. And on top of everything else, I finally took the test.

It was immediately positive. Immediately. I sank to the floor, trying to make sense of how quickly my life was falling apart. Everything at once failing the most critical class in my program, a positive pregnancy test, and a boyfriend who was already smiling before I could even process what I was looking at.

I didn't ask him what he thought. I already knew what I thought, and I said it before he could offer an opinion: I can't do this. I have to retake A&P and apply to nursing school. This is not the plan.

And with that, the decision was made. *Alone*: Before I consulted anyone. Before I prayed. Before I asked God what He thought about any of it. I was eighteen years old, raised in the Church of God in Christ—a denomination where a baby out of wedlock meant something very specific about who you were and where you were headed.

But I also had a plan. And in that moment, the plan felt more real to me than anything else.

He was excited. I want to be honest about that. He already had children from a previous relationship that had not gone well, and I think he could see something in me and in us that made him hopeful about what we could build. He had a plan too—and I was part of it. But he didn't say much when I told him what I had decided. He knew. He did not question it.

I didn't tell anyone else. But my mom knew something was wrong. Mothers always know. She cornered me, the way only a mother can. I was eighteen and technically an adult, but I also could not carry it alone for one more day. So I told her. She wasn't angry about the pregnancy itself—what hurt her was that I hadn't come to her first. She wanted to support me. She wanted to be in it with me. And I had shut her out because I was too ashamed to let her in. Too embarrassed that my attempt at being grown had produced the one thing I wasn't ready for.

She was more disappointed that I hadn't talked to her than she was about anything else. I carried that decision like a stone for years. Not because anyone loaded it onto me—but because I put it there and I kept it there. I knew what I had done. I knew why I had done it. I knew that the Lord knew too. And for a long time, I did not know how to hold all three of those things at once.

＊ ＊ ＊

Still, life kept moving, the way it always does. Despite the weight I carried, I couldn't pause.

I walked into the financial aid office shortly after, with what I can only now describe as a combination of audacity and grace I had absolutely not earned. My scholarship was being pulled because my GPA had dropped after I failed A&P. My appeal: I was working two jobs, stretched thin, and needed another chance. I faked the confidence I did not feel and made my case.

It worked.

I kept my scholarship. I retook A&P and earned the "B" I needed. I moved forward. And as I began to move forward, I also began to lean into God in a way I hadn't before—not a dramatic conversion, not a sudden transformation, but a slow and deliberate turning toward Him that started to give me new language for what I had been carrying.

I learned what repentance actually meant. Not just regret—but the act of turning, of releasing, of letting God reclaim what I had tried to handle alone. I had a lukewarm relationship with the Lord up to that point. Close enough to feel His presence when I needed something. Not close enough to surrender the steering wheel. But as I began to lean in, I started learning a lesson that would take me most of my twenties and into my thirties to fully absorb: I was His daughter. He had plans to prosper me. And I needed to release—really release—my grip on how I thought those plans were supposed to look and when they were supposed to arrive. I would have to learn that lesson again and again before it finally settled in me.

By the time nursing school was wrapping up, I had also been quietly coming to terms with the relationship I had been in since I was seventeen. He had carried me through four years of school in the most practical sense—the car, the flashcards, the gas, the steady presence. That kind of faithfulness meant something real to me. But faithfulness and stability are not the same thing as right. And I was growing in the things of God, while he was not growing with me.

I began to learn the language of soul ties—the way you can be so deeply bonded to someone that leaving them feels like cutting off part of yourself, even when you know it is what God is asking. The process of breaking up with him was not clean or easy. We had started living together by then, and we had shared something real for years. But I could not allow a good thing to keep me from a great thing. He didn't understand the covenant the way I needed him to. He didn't share my faith, nor did he want to. And I had seen enough of what a two-parent household built on a foundation of faith could look like to know that was what God had for me.

So, I left. And I grieved that quietly too—another loss tucked into the years before the story I thought I was living finally began.

* * *

The next few years, I started working as a nurse—living my single life, going out with my girls on weekends, loving on my niece who had become the joy of that season—when I met my first husband.

He presented everything I had been praying for. He was kind. He knew the Lord—not as deeply as I had hoped, but sincerely. He had a sense of humor. He had a life plan, even if he didn't yet have all the tools to execute it. He came from a two-parent household, which to me meant he at least had a foundational understanding of what a covenant looked like from the inside. I was still growing in God myself, so I extended the kind of grace I felt I had received: he doesn't have everything figured out yet, but neither do I. We'll grow together. God can work with this.

What I did not fully sit with was the inner knowing I had even before we married. It wasn't loud. It wasn't dramatic. It was quiet and certain and very easy to talk myself out of, because I was still young enough in my faith to second-guess whether I was hearing God or simply afraid of something good. I had an inner knowing I should not marry this man. And I moved forward anyway.

I want to be honest about that, because I think it matters. Not as a confession of failure—but as a witness to what it costs when we hear the Lord and choose our own timing anyway. I had been in the things of the world. I had done what I wanted to do. And I was still learning, really learning, that God's voice is not something you override when it's inconvenient. That lesson was still in process when I said yes.

We had the wedding of my dreams. One hundred and fifty people. A DJ, a formal sit-down dinner, a dance floor, a huge wedding party, a photographer, a honeymoon—all of it. Everything I had pictured. And for a while, we built something that looked like real life. We did ministry together. We found a community. We bought a house. We had rhythms and routines that felt solid from the outside.

But there were things I noticed along the way. Quiet things. Red flags about his readiness to lead, to initiate, to carry the weight that a husband and a household require. When I saw those things clearly, I was vocal about it—and, if I'm being honest, young Sylvia did not have much grace for a husband who struggled. I believed in excellence. I believed the Holy Spirit lived inside of us, and we didn't get to be mediocre. And that conviction, unchecked by mercy, made me a wife who was carrying more than her share and resenting him for it rather than building him up.

Nobody talks about what it means to have to lift the head of your house while he is down. The Bible says a virtuous woman does her husband good all the days of her life—even before she meets him, and when he is struggling. I was not doing that. I was managing. Leading. Compensating. And calling it strength.

We had been trying to have a baby for five years. Five years of hoping, of months that ended in disappointment, of a longing that didn't quiet down, no matter how much I tried to hand it to God. When IVF became the next option, I was ready to move.

In January, a close friend—someone I trusted deeply, who had become like a first lady to me—met me at an urgent care where I was sick with a fever. I was telling her about the IVF appointment I was already planning. She listened to my whole spiel—all the excitement, all the certainty that this was finally going to be the thing—and when I finished, she looked at me with a straight face and said: I think you should wait until March.

No explanation. No elaboration. Just that. My ears were hurting. My throat was sore. I had a final the next morning, and everything inside of me was already accelerating toward the appointment I had decided I was going to make. There was one IVF opening in February. One in April. I took the February appointment.

Be anxious for nothing—I knew the Scripture. I simply did not apply it. Everything I had been praying for felt like it was finally within reach, and I was not willing to slow down for one more month. I was tired of waiting. I had waited long enough. And I convinced myself that surely God understood that.

On March 14, 2015, I woke up with a plan to decorate my home for a coworker's baby shower. This was not just any shower—this was a woman I had walked alongside as she chose to keep her baby rather than end her pregnancy. I had shared my own story with her to help her make that decision. I had become that baby's godmother. The celebration mattered deeply to me. I had a onesie station planned, a diaper cake, a specific food arrangement, and the games. I knew exactly where everything was going.

At 9:32 in the morning, I felt a migraine coming on. I noted the time—I would understand later why the Holy Spirit had me fix my eyes on that clock. I decided to pause, eat some breakfast, take my medicine, and start fresh. I took out the turkey bacon because I wanted people to know I was healthy. No high blood pressure. Normal cholesterol. No pre-existing conditions that would have predicted what was about to happen. I was twenty-nine years old and completely healthy by every measure medicine had to offer.

As I stood at the refrigerator, I felt the left side of my face fall. I reached up with my fingers to try to lift it back into place. I did not know I was having a stroke.

What followed happened fast. Weakness on the left side. Then the entire left side of my body. Then my speech disappeared—completely. I could understand everything being said to me, every word, every question, and when I tried to respond, what came out of my mouth was gibberish. My then-husband called 911. The paramedics arrived and began asking me assessment questions. I knew what they were doing—I was a nurse, and I recognized a neurological assessment. I knew the early bird gets the worm. And when I tried to say it, I heard it clearly in my mind and heard something completely unrecognizable come out of my mouth.

Something is happening. I could not name it. Stroke was not a category my brain would place me in. I was twenty-nine years old. I was otherwise healthy. It did not compute.

At the hospital, the initial CT scan—done without contrast— came back clear. The bedside nurse started printing discharge paperwork. And that is when my cousin, who had built a career as a certified nursing assistant, stepped in and requested a CT with contrast.

There it was. A blood clot lodged in my right middle cerebral artery. I had already missed the window for clot-busting medication. The clot was removed through a minimally invasive procedure—no head incision was required. The faithfulness of God was in every single detail of that sequence: the cousin who knew what to ask for, the doctor who listened, the delay that led to the right scan at the right moment.

I believe the IVF hormones, layered on top of the graduate school stress I was carrying at the time, caused the clot. Had I waited until March—as my friend had told me to in that urgent care parking lot—I do not believe I would have had that stroke. I did not wait. And I have spent years learning how to accept what that cost me.

Chapter 3

Renee's Story

"When Love Finally Finds You"

I grew up in a household where independence wasn't a choice—it was just how things worked. My mom raised my brother and me largely on her own, working two jobs. We spent a lot of time at home without her, so I stepped into a caretaker role early. I made sure we ate, got up for school, and that the morning ran smoothly. We figured things out and managed. We became the kind of kids who didn't need to be told twice, because we knew what to do and took care of things.

What I remember most from those years isn't resentment—it's the longing for structure. I wanted guidance. And without it, I became very good at guiding myself. I was navigating things far too early on my own and taking care of other people, including my parents. What I still haven't learned is how to take care of myself. Not in the basic ways I was most certainly great at, but in my emotions and feelings.

* * *

By the time I was a teenager, we had moved around quite a bit. When I landed in Denton and started middle school there, something had shifted—not just in my circumstances, but in me.

I had spent years being the responsible one. The quiet one. The one who held things together while quietly carrying a need I couldn't fully name. During that period, as I fulfilled these roles, I gradually became aware of a deeper longing: to be known. Not just needed—*known*. Chosen. I wanted to be seen for something beyond what I could do for everyone else.

That longing didn't announce itself. It just started shaping decisions before I understood that's what it was doing. I found myself in situations I wasn't equipped for, making choices without the tools or guidance that should have come long before. No one was watching closely enough to set boundaries, and I didn't yet know how to set them for myself. So I moved through those years the only way I knew how—figuring it out as I went. I was carrying more than I should have, and slowly collecting a belief I wouldn't examine for years: love was something you earned by making yourself available to it. That being chosen came with a cost. And that the cost was worth paying if it meant someone stayed. It wasn't. And they didn't. But I didn't know that yet.

* * *

I met the man who would become Myriah's father, my first child, at the apartment complex right next to the one we lived in. Back then, everyone hung out outside—friends from school, guys playing basketball, people just hanging out the way people do in apartment complexes. However, he was ten years older than me. I never lied about my age. He knew I was sixteen, and we both knew no one in their right mind would approve of our relationship, so we didn't ask. It was our secret.

My brother figured it out first. He noticed I kept disappearing, and one day, he followed me. He told my mom. And even after that came to light, the situation just continued—nothing substantial changed, and there were no real consequences that stopped it.

Within a few months, I was pregnant with Myriah.

Before I told anyone, I tried to handle it on my own. I was sixteen—just a child. I couldn't navigate it without a parent and was running out of ways to keep it quiet. Eventually, I couldn't hide it anymore. When I finally told my mom, I had already decided: I wanted to keep my baby and face everything that came with it. It was settled in me before anyone else weighed in, and I knew I would take care of her, just as I always had. Nine months later, I had my baby girl.

* * *

After Myriah was born, my life became something I had to build in real time, day by day. In high school, there was a program for teen moms that provided support, including rides to and from school, as well as supplies and resources. The bus would pick me up at five in the morning. I would get on the bus with Myriah, drop her at daycare, go to school, come back, pick her up, and do it all over again. That was the shape of my days. No complaining. No time to process. Just survival—the same mode I had been operating in since I was old enough to make sure my brother got on the bus.

Eventually, things didn't work out between Myriah's dad and me. He moved away, and I found myself back with just my mom and my brother, now with a child of my own. Not long after, my mom decided to move to Houston. And just like that, I was seventeen with a one-year-old, figuring life out completely on my own now.

I graduated one year early and started working. My best friend Amber and I got an apartment together—me, her, and Myriah. And life started to settle. I found another rhythm, an easier one, and got comfortable with our new normal. Eventually, time passed, and I found someone new after about two years.

I met him online. We had finally arranged a meeting in person; he came to visit Myriah and me, and from that point on, we were together almost every day. He had a daughter of his own and fully accepted mine. For the first time, something felt like a family. He showed up in ways Myriah's dad never had. I held onto that, because I wasn't just looking for love—I was looking for someone to do life with. Someone who would stay.

But wanting something to work and actually having it work are two different things. Especially when you are young. Things fell apart between us quietly. By the time I found out I was pregnant again, we weren't together. I remember taking the test. Positive. Again.

When I told him, he hesitated—rightfully so; we were not monogamous. Just like that, things went silent. For nine months, I went through pregnancy alone. Just me, again, carrying something enormous by myself.

After I had Myrisa, we did a DNA test. She was proven his, and from that day, he stepped up as a father—always present, willing to show up for her. But our relationship never recovered. We tried again briefly, even moved back in together for a season, but it didn't last. We went our separate ways for good.

I was a single mother of two daughters, each with a different father. I had no real sense of what a healthy relationship looked like. But I wasn't bitter. I didn't hate men. I didn't even lose hope. I had never really built expectations in the first place—never dreamed about a wedding, never imagined a fairy tale. I just knew I didn't want to be alone. So, even when relationships ended, the feeling that lingered wasn't despair, but always a quiet, persistent hope beneath everything: that one day I would find my person. That one day, I would build something I had never actually seen done right.

* * *

My best friend Amanda had gotten married to a guy named Mike, and we were around each other often. Mike overheard many of the failed dating conversations I shared with Amanda. One day, out of nowhere, Mike said he was going to give his brother, Corey, my number. Immediately, I declined, but he did it anyway.

Little did I know that my life would change forever after one phone call.

Not long after, my phone rang with a number I didn't recognize. When I answered, it was Corey. He was silly and not shy at all. Completely opposite of myself. But, I thought to myself, what is the worst that could happen? I'll entertain this attention for a while.

I didn't take it seriously at first. If anything, I thought he was completely out of my league. He went to church. I had been to church here and there with my grandmother, but nothing consistent as I grew up. I didn't have a relationship with God—I didn't know what that meant. I had two daughters by two different men, and in my mind, there was simply no way someone like him would actually want someone like me. But he kept calling.

The first time we saw each other in person after talking on the phone was at the hospital when Amanda had her baby. I was there for her. He was there because it was his niece. As we all watched Amanda hold the new baby close to her skin, we learned about the importance of skin-to-skin. Corey, being the fun, lighthearted person he was, grabbed my arm and made a joke about doing skin-to-skin and giving him a hug—that was the icebreaker. Everybody started laughing. And just like that, whatever distance or question in my mind about the possibility of him and me dissipated. I realized we were just two people who genuinely liked each other, and if I was enough for him, I was definitely going to accept it.

Dating him felt different from anything I had experienced before. He wasn't bothered by my past or by the fact that I had two daughters. He was naturally good with them—instinctively, without trying. And that mattered to me more than I probably understood at the time.

At first, I thought he was corny—a church boy, not my type. But that changed. I started falling for him and knew I would marry him, even before we were official. I just knew.

He eventually got his own apartment, which gave us actual space to build something. I would go over there with the girls. He would come visit us. We started doing life things together—normal, steady, real. It started to feel like something I could actually trust.

He invited me to church. I went. And I sat there completely out of place—not because anyone made me feel unwelcome, but because I genuinely did not know that world. I didn't know God like that. I didn't understand the language or what any of it meant for my life. I just knew it was different, and I wasn't sure where I fit in it. But I kept going back. Because he was there, and because something in that environment felt like it was pointing toward something I hadn't been able to name yet.

I didn't know he would become a pastor. He was just someone who served, someone who occasionally taught on student Sundays. There was no big picture in my mind. All I knew was this: for the first time in my life, something felt steady. Something felt safe. Something felt like it could actually last. And I leaned into that with everything I had. Because after everything I had lived through,

I wasn't looking for perfection. I was just looking for something that was for *me*, for *real*.

* * *

Over time, things got serious, and everything changed. It was around Valentine's, and Corey was taking Myriah to a daddy-daughter dance. He had told my family in advance, but I had no idea what was coming. He came to the door with a rose for her, smiling bigger than usual. I remembered thinking to myself, "*Why is he so happy?*"

We walked outside together. Myriah was exuding happiness, feeling a love she had never known from a man. Smiling from ear to ear. Nearby, a limo was parked and waiting. She was completely shocked. Then Corey got down on one knee as family and friends began stepping out of the limo. Meanwhile, I just stood there thinking, "*What is happening right now*?!"

When he proposed, I was completely shocked. I had never dreamed about being proposed to. I had never planned a wedding in my head. So when it happened, it felt surreal—like something that happened to other people, people who had grown up expecting it. But here it was, happening to me.

We planned our wedding in about four months. We didn't over-complicate it—I had never been the type to dream about a wedding, so I didn't come with a long list of expectations. We just wanted to get married, and soon. It turned out beautiful. Our friends and family were there, and Corey's family embraced me and my girls without a moment's hesitation. They loved us as we had always been theirs. No questions, no conditions, no adjustment period. Just love, immediate and full.

It felt like a fairytale. Which was something I had never once allowed myself to imagine for my life. After the honeymoon—a cruise—we came back and started our life together. I was growing in my career while we were growing as a family. Everything felt stable. The girls loved Corey, and he treated them like they were his own—completely, without qualification.

Corey walked me into a real relationship with God. Not through pressure or expectation, but through living it out beside me, in the way he led our home and loved our family. I began to develop a faith of my own—not inherited from anyone else, but something that grew in me as I watched what it looked like when someone truly knew God. We decided to buy a house, trusted God with it, and when we moved in, it felt like stepping into something solid. Not long after, we found out we were pregnant with CJ. Bringing him home to that house felt like I had made it in life. Whatever that means.

We were building the life I had never let myself imagine. But behind the scenes, things were beginning to shift. Corey was stepping deeper into church leadership—his grandfather had passed, and Corey had taken on a major role in carrying what was left behind. He was a husband, a father, and now a pastor, and it was all landing on him at once. The stress showed up first as chest pain. We brushed it off—he had a lot on his plate. He even took a trip to Florida to spend time with a mentor, just to reset. But when he came back, things didn't fully settle.

One morning, he woke up feeling like he couldn't breathe. We drove straight to the emergency room. They ran tests and did an EKG. Everything looked fine. But the symptoms kept coming back. By 2020, they had escalated. He began seeing a cardiologist. He had episodes where he didn't feel like he was breathing right. One time, it scared him enough that he drove himself to the hospital. Tests came back normal again. But we both knew something wasn't right.

When they ran his bloodwork, the picture changed. His troponin levels were extremely high, which meant there had already been some kind of event with his heart. They ordered additional testing procedures where they inject dye to track blood flow through the arteries. That's when they discovered the blockages.

By July 2020, we were sitting with the reality that Corey needed triple bypass surgery. I was in complete shock. And the world was in the middle of a pandemic—COVID. The hospital was locked down. Corey was admitted, and I could barely be there. His parents couldn't come. Our kids couldn't come. It was just us: navigating one of the hardest things we'd faced together, in complete isolation from the people who would have surrounded us. Even then, I kept telling myself: it's just surgery. He's going to be fine. We're going to get through this.

He had the surgery, but the restrictions tightened further during his recovery. There were days I couldn't be there at all. But I held onto the same belief: this is just our challenge. We're going to overcome it.

For a while, it looked like that might be true. He was recovering. Walking. Adjusting. But something still wasn't right. The chest pain continued. And then one day, he had another episode and went back to the hospital.

All three of the grafts from his bypass surgery had failed. I didn't even know that was possible. Now they were recommending a left main stent—a critical artery, a serious and high-risk placement. We were back in the hospital. I stayed in the same mindset: okay, this is the next step. We'll do this and move forward. He had the stent placed. We went home again, trying to return to normal. But underneath everything, there was a quiet tension that wouldn't settle. We were walking into something we didn't yet understand.

* * *

On Saturday, January 1, 2021, we drove out to visit my grandfather, who lives in East Texas. When we arrived, Corey seemed like himself—a little quieter than usual, maybe, but that wasn't unusual. He could fall asleep anywhere, any time. He mentioned he hadn't taken his medication that day and hadn't even brought it with him. Still, he didn't act like anything was wrong.

What happened while we were there is something I carry with me to this day. My grandfather has always known God, but he has never been the type to consistently go to church or live out his faith openly. That day, he asked Corey to step outside and talk with him alone. When Corey came back in, he told me that my grandfather had been carrying unforgiveness in his heart. He wanted to be free from it. Corey walked him through it—talked about forgiveness, led him in prayer, and prayed a prayer of salvation with him. That memory means more to me now than I have words for.

We eventually left and headed home. The next day was Sunday, January 2—the first Sunday of the new year and the first Sunday we reopened our church for in-person services after months of COVID restrictions. It felt like a significant moment.

On the way home, we dropped Myriah off at a skating rink for a student event. Corey wanted a haircut before church the next morning, so I dropped him off at the barbershop. Before I left, he mentioned he wasn't feeling that great. I drove home to get his medication. While I was gone, he called to say someone at the barbershop had given him some Advil. When I got back, I gave him his medicine. He finished his haircut. We headed home. On the way, he asked for Panda Express, so we picked up dinner. Once we got home, everyone was relaxed—eating, playing cards, spending time together. My brother and his wife were with us. It felt like a normal night.

At some point, my brother said something to his wife, and Corey playfully stepped in, poking him in the head, telling him not to talk to her like that. They started playing wrestling—the way they always did. My brother is bigger than Corey, but Corey managed to pick him up and throw him onto the couch. Then Corey stood up and said, *"My chest. My chest!"*

He lifted his arms above his head, trying to catch his breath. I was sitting by the fireplace watching, and at first, I wasn't alarmed. By that point, these episodes had started to feel familiar—like something he would push through the way he always did. But my sister-in-law knew something was different. She ran to the car to get his medication. Corey followed her out to the garage.

Then I heard her scream my name. I ran out and saw him going down. I don't even know how I got him to the ground, but suddenly I was there, holding him, trying to understand what was happening. I grabbed my phone, called 911, and started CPR.

Everything after that felt like both seconds and hours at the same time. My sister-in-law was trying to keep the kids inside. My brother was sitting against the garage wall, crying, apologizing over and over. I kept telling him it was okay. He was going to be fine. I believed that. I tried to get Corey's nitro into his mouth, but his jaw was clenched shut. I couldn't get it open. He wasn't responding.

I kept going. When the police arrived, they took over CPR and told me to go inside. They loaded him into the ambulance. Someone told me there wasn't a heartbeat—but there was still something. *Something* they were holding onto. So, I held onto it too.

We all gathered and prayed together before I left. Then I went to the hospital. I remember sitting there, waiting. His parents arrived. Everything felt suspended—as time had stopped, but also like it was moving too fast.

Then they called us into a room. A doctor started asking questions about the day, about what led up to the moment. His mom interrupted, asking directly, "What's going on?" And in that moment, he stopped trying to ease into it.

He just said: "He's gone."

I didn't want to go see him. I was too scared. I had never experienced anything like this before. I don't even remember crying at that moment. I was in complete shock. Everything felt unreal. Like I had stepped out of my life and into something I didn't recognize. I left the hospital that day and went home to a life that would never be the same again.

Chapter 4

Nakeisha's Story

"Left Behind"

My mother's disappearance happened in phases. At first, she would be gone for a few hours and then make her way back. That happened often enough that we stayed in the mindset of oh, she'll be back soon. A few hours turned into overnight. Overnight turned into a couple of days. The leaving was so gradual that I couldn't even point to a specific day when I realized she wasn't coming back. It just kept stacking up until one day we looked around, and it had been a while. And then the utilities started getting turned off. We stayed outside until we couldn't anymore. And then we would sit in the apartment in the dark.

I remember the first night the lights went off. The immediate thought was, "What are we going to do?" We were both kids. How long could we actually do this? My little brother was younger than me, but he stepped into a role no child should have to—going out into the neighborhood, talking to people he knew, figuring out how to get food or where we could spend the night. The crowd around us at that time was mostly people just trying to survive however they could, drug dealers and folks doing what they had to do, and those were the connections we had available to us. Some nights we sat in that apartment with flashlights. Other nights, my brother would talk our way into a friend's place in the complex, convincing their parents to let us stay over.

And I was still going to school during that time. Not every day—but enough. School was genuinely one of the places I wanted to be. I liked learning. I liked being around my friends. I was a nerd, and I say that without any apology. Even in the middle of everything falling apart at home, the school environment still made sense to me. When my friends decided they weren't going on a particular day, I had options. And sometimes I took them. But school was one of the few things that gave my days some kind of shape when nothing else did.

I never thought about calling anyone for help. Not once. My entire mindset was that I didn't want my mom to get in trouble. I didn't want us to be separated or taken somewhere. I didn't want the system involved in our lives. And if I am being completely honest, there was also a strange kind of freedom in how we were living. Before she left, the rules were the normal ones every parent has: *Come home before the streetlights come on. Do your homework before you go outside. Finish your dinner.* The regular things. Once she stopped coming back, those rules disappeared with her. We were just kids in a neighborhood doing what we wanted. No curfew. No accountability. In the way that only children can rationalize things, we were living our best lives.

But underneath that freedom was something neither of us had words for yet. We were completely on our own. And we were thirteen and younger. And the world around us was not designed to protect us.

We had always gone to Prayer of Faith—our mom had made sure of that, even though she rarely set foot in a church herself. That church was where we had built the relationships that would eventually carry us. *Cynthia. Weldon. Aunt Tanya. Aunt Sheila.* These were people who had known us for years. But even with that community in the background, the day-to-day survival still fell on my brother and me. We made it work because we had to. Because no one was coming to do it for us. That was the first thing abandonment taught me. You can wait for someone to come back, or you can figure out how to move. We chose to move.

* * *

I was a freshman in high school when I got pregnant. By that point, we had been managing life on our own long enough that it had started to feel like the only way life worked. My brother handled the survival logistics. I kept showing up to school when I could. And somewhere in the middle of all of that, I started seeing someone—older, already out of school, part of the crowd we ran with on the days we skipped. There was no grand love story behind it. We were young and close to each other, and that was most of it. He knew what he was doing, and I didn't, and the first time I had sex with him, I ended up pregnant.

I didn't know right away. I never really got morning sickness, and I was thick enough that the early changes weren't visible to me or anyone else. What tipped me off was my cycle stopping. I had a close friend at the time who had already been through pregnancy herself—she'd had a couple of kids, and she recognized signs that I was too inexperienced to read. She pulled me aside and said she thought I might be pregnant. We went and got a test. It came back positive.

The first feeling was automatic—*I'm gonna get in trouble.* That's exactly where your mind goes when you're young, and something like that happens. But the second thought came right behind it, and it landed differently. My mom wasn't there. There was no one to get in trouble with. So it stopped being about getting caught and became about figuring out what we were going to do, because we were the only ones who would figure it out.

So, I hid my pregnancy for as long as I could. I made it seven and a half months before any adult found out. The only people who knew were a few of my friends, whom I trusted to keep quiet. I went to school. I went about my life. I was managing the way I had learned to manage everything else—quietly, without asking for help, without drawing attention to something that would change everything the moment anyone knew.

What gave me away was a volleyball game. I was jumping around on that court, and things started showing that weren't supposed to show. I got pulled from the game and taken directly to the principal's office. The nurse came in. The questions started. Does your mom know? Does anyone know? Is there an adult in your life we can contact?

No. You are the first adults to find out.

I sat in that office at seven and a half months pregnant and watched them try to reach my mother and fail. Eventually, they tracked down our Uncle David. My brother and I were going to have to go live with him.

I don't know if I felt relief or dread at that moment. Probably both. A lot of the time with my uncle is blurry for me now. I think I blocked portions of it out on purpose, the way your mind protects you from things it doesn't want to carry in full detail.

What I remember most clearly is the pressure. His message was direct and consistent: I was too young to be a parent. There was no way I could take care of a baby. I didn't have the resources, the support, or the maturity to do it. If I were going to live under his roof, the expectation was that I would have an abortion and move on. He had children of his own, but they were grown or living elsewhere. He was not interested in absorbing what I was carrying into his household.

I told the baby's father I was getting an abortion, because at that point, I genuinely believed that was what was going to happen. That was the last real conversation we had about it. He never found out otherwise. He went on with his life, not knowing what actually happened.

Even while we were living with my uncle, we were still finding our way back to the Prayer of Faith. That church had been the constant in our lives, even when nothing else was. Cynthia and Weldon were there. Aunt Tanya and Aunt Sheila were there. These people had known us since we were small, and when the news spread that I was pregnant and in a complicated situation, the community gathered around us the way communities of faith do.

But gathering around me also meant making decisions for me. The adults put together a plan. The best thing for everyone, they decided, would be for me to give the baby up for adoption. Not a formal legal adoption to strangers—there was a couple in the church I thought of as family, and the arrangement was that they would raise my son. I would still be able to see him. I just wouldn't be his mother in any official sense. And even though it was not what I wanted—even though something in me was already saying no, this is *mine*—that was the plan the adults had built for me while I sat nearby.

✳ ✳ ✳

The church threw me a baby shower. And at that shower, the pastor's daughter pulled me to the side. Her name was Lasunda, and she had been a young mother herself. She knew what it was to be in my position—young, overwhelmed, surrounded by people who thought they knew better. She looked at me and said the words I needed someone to say out loud: "*You don't have to do this if it is not what you want.*" She didn't tell me it would be easy. She didn't sugarcoat anything. But she told me clearly that nobody could force me to give my baby away. I had a voice. I had the right to use it. And the decision was mine to make.

That conversation cracked something open in me. I had spent so much of my life being moved by circumstances—moved by my mother's addiction, moved by survival, moved by whatever adults decided was best. I had gotten very good at adapting to whatever was in front of me. But this was different. This was *my* child. And for the first time, someone gave me permission to say what I actually wanted: I wanted to keep my son. So I said it. Out loud. To the people who had been making plans around me. And that was the end of the adoption conversation.

* * *

Cynthia and Weldon stepped in and took both my brother and me into their home.

They already had a full house—a lot of children, a lot of shared space, a system that had to flex to accommodate two more people, and eventually a newborn. At first, it was wherever there was room. The living room. A spot in one of the kids' rooms. Slowly, they reorganized things so the boys had a room, and the girls had a room. It wasn't fancy. It wasn't perfect. But it was structured, warm, and more than we had been living with. By that point, I was near the end of my pregnancy, and sleeping in a bed had become uncomfortable no matter which way I turned. Most nights, I ended up in a recliner. My body had outgrown the ordinary options.

My son was two weeks overdue. No signs of him coming on his own. I was scheduled for a C-section. But the day before, we had all gone together to a funeral—the whole church family, all of us in one place the way we always were. Afterward, Aunt Sheila refused to take me to the hospital without feeding me first. She could not in good conscience send me in there hungry, she said. So, we stopped and got food. Wrong decision.

That meal sent me straight into labor. By the time we got to the hospital, there was no need for induction or any of the preparations they had planned. Labor had already started on its own. Aunt Sheila, Aunt Tanya, and Cynthia were all with me—they had all been at the funeral, so they were already together, and they all came. It felt, in that strange and overwhelming way, like being surrounded by people who genuinely loved me. It didn't change the fact that I was fifteen years old and about to become a mother. But it made the room feel less terrifying.

It took three days for my son to arrive. I went in on a Friday and labored all day. Saturday, they stopped everything so I could eat, rest, and recover some strength. Sunday, the process started again. When we finally got to the end, the doctors had to use forceps to help get him out, which added a layer of fear to an already intense situation. But he was healthy. The delivery was successful. When it was finally over, and they placed him in my arms, reality settled in the way it can only settle in that kind of moment. I was fifteen years old. And now I had a person to take care of.

Chapter 5

Chas' Story

"When Survival Chooses"

Nobody tells you what happens after survival. Nobody tells you that when you finally get out, when you finally find someone who says they want you, that you will run toward them so fast you won't stop to ask whether they're safe.

You won't ask questions. You won't slow down. You won't even check yourself. Because all you know is this: This has to be better than what I just came out of.

That was me. I didn't grow up with stability. I grew up constantly adjusting. Moving from environment to environment…each environment with different family dynamics, different morals and values. So, of course, different rules, different expectations.

I became a chameleon, young, perfect Patty was the name. Failure was never an option. And if I'm honest, after a while, numbness felt the safest. I constantly had to learn how to exist in spaces that never quite felt like mine. I had fragments of homes, pieces of people, and seasons that didn't last long enough to feel secure. So somewhere along the way, my body learned something before my mind ever could: *If you want people to stay, you make yourself easy to keep.*

So I did just that. I learned how to read a room before I would ever speak. I learned how to shift my tone, depending on who I was around. I learned to silence my needs so no one else would feel uncomfortable. People-pleasing wasn't a personality trait for me. It was my makeup. It was survival. Because in my mind, disappointment led to distance, and distance felt like abandonment.

Time, after time, after time, I bent. I bent so much, I didn't even know where I ended, and other people began. That version of me walked straight into my first real relationship. It was good until it wasn't. He was safe, and feeling safe was important to me. However, he was taking me nowhere quickly. That relationship ended after two years, and I entered another relationship shortly after.

At first, it felt like love. Familiarity has a way of doing that. It makes things feel safe when they really aren't. We connected. We spent lots of time together. We talked about starting a family and what our future would look like. He went so far as to give me a blueprint of our future home. Stability captured my heart. And for a moment, I believed I had found something steady. This was the one I was supposed to spend my entire life with. But then, life happened. He lost his father—right in front of our eyes. We lost our unborn son, not long after. And something in him changed.

He began drinking heavily. He was not who he had always been. I no longer felt safe—I was deeply afraid. All of that softness turned into meanness. His presence turned into unpredictability. His words cut me in ways that didn't just hurt; they reshaped how I saw myself. I found myself trying to prove that I was worth loving, instead of asking why I had to prove anything at all.

I navigated all of this while trying to press my way to graduate high school and get to college. And although I made it through, it wasn't long before I failed out of college and lost everything I'd worked so hard for, chasing the very thing that meant no good. I was too blind to see that the fear of abandonment had me in a chokehold, and I was willing to keep what little bit of stability I had at any cost. But *boyyy, did I pay the cost…*

I'd failed out of college and was barely surviving. I had also found myself pregnant again. I was afraid because technically, we were no longer together. If I'm honest, parts of me felt free, but somehow, there were still parts of me that smiled at the thought of us being a family.

I rehearsed the lines over and over again of the way I'd tell him. *Maybe this will make him love me differently. Maybe this will make him truly choose me again.* Those were the thoughts that were going through my mind. When I called him over to tell him, I expected something to shift. What actually happened changed me.

He told me he had twins on the way with someone else. I remember standing there, holding my own reality while everything around me collapsed at the same time. Shock didn't even feel like the right word. It was deeper than that. And then came the words he spoke with that spiteful grin of his:

That I was stupid.

That I was desperate.

That I would never be enough for him or for anyone else.

I could feel everything rising in me. Everything I wanted to say. Everything I wanted to do. But I didn't. I swallowed it. Because that's what I knew how to do. Endure. Yet, that night, I found pieces of courage and boldness. I found the strength to finally walk away—completely. I packed everything I could fit into my little Mazda Sport. I gave my roommate my keys and what I had left for rent. And I left. No announcement. No true explanation. I got on the highway heading east, and I didn't look back.

When I got to my destination, I didn't heal — I wasn't even trying to. I hid…and I slept. All day. All night. I avoided people. I avoided conversations. I avoided anything that required me to feel. Life had been so hard without explanation—I was so undeserving of all of the pain, and I just felt like I didn't want to do or be anything anymore. I had fallen into a depression I didn't know how to come out of. No one really knew where I was except my father and my grandmother. And honestly…I didn't care—I didn't want to be found.

It was in my place of hiding that my Ken entered my story—DJ Ken Deezy was what they called him. My god-sister asked me to drive her to the store one day — I did it grudgingly. Little did I know this day would change the trajectory of my life.

Entering the store were two male contractors working for Eckerd's, and lo and behold, one was Ken. He was on a ladder doing some wiring and kept trying to make me laugh. Eventually, he did.

That laughter was the medicine I didn't even know I needed. When you've been carrying heaviness for so long, even a small moment of lightness can feel safe. He invited me out to this club. I didn't know that meeting him at this club was actually me walking into the beginning of what was going to be the best parts of my life.

He chose me, and that was enough for me. But to know he chose me when I was not at my best nor at my strongest made my heart feel again. He came in steady. He carried weight that never belonged to him. I never had to question his intentions. His presence was a safe place. He made it easy for me to want to love again.

And then one day, out of the blue, he looked at me and said that he was going to make me his wife. That was the nail that sealed our fate. We didn't ease into life together. We collided into it.

Children.

Responsibility.

Expectations.

All immediately, and all at once. It was all fun and games until it wasn't. I was stepping into roles I wasn't prepared for. Bonus mom, specifically. Ken was a full-time dad when I met him, having been one for about 3 years. There was a level of responsibility he had that I wasn't used to, and it was scary to think that every decision I would now make in life had to consider a child's well-being. I remember moments when the weight of it all would hit me, and I'd think to myself, "*This is heavier than I expected.*" But I wouldn't dare say it. I didn't want to fail. I realized quickly that I wasn't the only one depending on his presence and consistency.

As our lives quickly unfolded, I was still trying to figure out who I was, and at the same time, who he was. Around the same time, we made the impulsive decision to move to Dallas because it was something he had always wanted to do. I was hesitant because of what I had just come out of, but I trusted him. I felt safe with him. It felt like another chance. Another reset. It felt like this time would be different.

We started making plans to build something that felt like stability. But almost as quickly as we started, life shifted again. I got pregnant with McKynzie. And shortly after that…we separated. What was once a breath of fresh air became rocky terrain and our first hurdle. Just like that. Everything we were trying to build was gone before it ever had a chance to stand. I was carrying life, while at the same time grieving what felt like the loss of ours. We had already started making life decisions together, trying to create something real. But we were young. Unstable. And building on a foundation that didn't exist. So, when things started falling apart, they didn't just shake, rattle, or crack; they collapsed.

Our credit took several hard hits early on. Mistakes stacked on top of mistakes, and we weren't prepared for the consequences. Four months apart from one another during the latter part of the pregnancy seemed to be extremely long and unbearable, as if I were carrying my child alone. There were moments I didn't even know how to feel.

I began to contemplate: "*Do I constantly replay the last words my ex spoke to me?*" Maybe it's true, I will never be enough. No man would ever have me as a wife—I'm damaged goods.

Should I become angry or sad?

Maybe I should hate him, or, honestly, hate myself.

Should I constantly live in fear?

Will McKynzie grow up without her father in her life?

Will I be that woman I never wanted to be?

What I was carrying was heavy—and it showed. April 21, 2004, McKynzie was born, and somehow her birth brought us back together. We were still wounded, but we still believed in what we were trying to build, even if we didn't quite know how to. After a few months of commuting back and forth to Dallas for visits, Ken came and packed McKynzie and me up.

From there, we moved back to Tyler. We had a few hurdles to jump to settle in, but once we did, for a moment, life felt so good. Although not on our own timeline, we got married. We were happy and healthily raising a blended family of three. We were learning how to co-parent well. We were truly just trying to create something that resembled normalcy. We could *breathe* again. It truly felt like we were getting it right—until we weren't.

I lost my job. Then he lost his. Once stability was gone, everything else followed. We lost our cars. We lost our home. And just like that…we were homeless. There's something about being in that position that strips every single part of you down.

Your pride.

Your plans.

Your expectations.

All of it. And what we realized in that season was something we hadn't faced yet. What we were building never had a foundation. It took effort. It had intention. It even had love. But it didn't have structure. And it definitely didn't have healing.

We were stuck in an endless cycle of trying and falling; then rebuilding and breaking. Over and over again, only to end up with us separated again. Seven months had gone by this time. But this time I fought for us, because I realized I hated being without him. He had become a piece of my makeup. There was no me without him.

We found our way back again. And almost immediately, I was pregnant with McKayla. You would think by then we would have learned something. Slowed down; maybe if we'd done things differently. But we didn't. We picked back up where we left off and ended up right back in a struggle. Right back in instability. Right back in survival. We were homeless again.

That's when my mom stepped in, angrily. She made me move back to Dallas. Not for me, but for the safety and stability of my one-year-old daughter and my unborn child, for whom I hadn't received any healthcare. She could see what we were too close to recognize…. We were repeating something we didn't know how to break out of.

Out of fear, real fear this time, of falling back into that same cycle again, my husband made a decision that changed the trajectory of all of our lives. He joined the military. It was never his dream. He didn't even choose his career path when he joined. He took whatever was available for stability's sake.

Fort Stewart, Georgia, was our duty station. We knew no one, but moving to Georgia felt like hope. It truly felt like home. I remember feeling seen by God. For the first time in my life, I had peace. Just like everything else in my life, that peace came with a cost.

Ken stepped into that life, and I slowly felt him drift. He had a purpose. He had family outside of the family we made. I felt left behind…at home, carrying everything else. I would sit on the sofa at night, after the kids went to sleep, in complete silence. And that silence felt cold. I would ask myself, *"Why am I never enough? Will I ever be?"*

The man who was supposed to be my best friend and hero has done the same thing that everyone else did to me—abandoned me. My life had immediately become a life lived in his shadow. And that kind of loneliness does something to you. It leaves you desperate, vulnerable, and empty. You crave adult conversation and attention after a while, and once you finally get it, you grab hold of it and try so hard not to let go.

No one could've ever told me that I would do the unthinkable—not "perfect patty." Turns out, I wasn't so perfect after all, and this was the very moment that knocked me into reality. What I thought was just a connection turned into something more. I wasn't trying to destroy my marriage at all; all I knew was that in a moment where I was feeling abandoned, trapped, empty, and suicidal, someone made me feel heard, valuable, seen, and appreciated.

The affair didn't start with an intention. It started with emptiness. It started with someone showing up in a space where I felt completely unseen. Of course, it came with a cost… and (story of my life) *boyyy, did I pay.*

After that, things were never the same. Something had shifted. We tried so hard to push through, but my husband just couldn't shake what he was feeling. That was the moment I learned that some things, once broken, won't ever go back the same way. The heaviness. The tension. I saw it in our children. And I knew then that we had passed something down that we didn't mean to.

The only way I knew to course correct was to file for divorce. Not because I didn't love him, but because I did. I saw the hurt in his eyes daily. I felt the thick moments of regret in the air when he was in his head. I would excuse certain behaviors at times because I knew just how bad I'd hurt him.

Although we had picked up the pieces, there was always resistance. His heart didn't pump at the same rate. His eyes never lit up the same way. I felt like he put his entire life on the line to carry a weight for me that he never had to, and I failed him. I let him down. I missed the mark. I was supposed to be different, and for years I was, until I wasn't. I felt like I no longer deserved him, and towards the end, he told me he didn't have it in him to fight for us. As bad as it hurt to hear those words, I felt like I deserved it.

I took the first step reluctantly, but it felt like he had already divorced me silently anyway. It was quiet. Heavy. Final. I could hardly breathe. My body was trembling. What made it harder was that we stayed in the same house throughout the entire process and for months after the divorce was final. The kids had no idea that their world was about to be turned upside down. I watched them, day in and day out, live their normal lives, and the entire time I knew everything was about to shift.

One day, McKynzie caught a whiff of what was happening, and I can never shake the damage it caused her. I still relive it in real time, sometimes knowing that there was nothing normal, safe, or stable about her upbringing. I was supposed to protect her from all the things I felt I wasn't protected from, and here I was failing her. I was disappointed in myself, not in anyone else.

Once the heaviness hit McKynzie, it sent a wave through our entire household. I faulted myself, not only for the divorce, but for tearing my family apart. The family I dedicated my entire life to was now in ruins. To know everyone's pain around you is centered on a decision you made is beyond unbearable. It became increasingly clear that we were no longer sleeping in the same bed or even being home at the same time.

The kids' behavior began to increase, not in a good way. Love began to look more like constant arguing between them all. I pondered, "*What have I done?*" I stressed over my decision, which could no longer be undone. I had stepped into something I knew I wasn't equipped to handle. I feared their future and mine.

Ken found an apartment locally and stayed in Georgia, while I chose to move back home to Texas. He moved out of our family home a week before I did, so packing up the U-Haul truck was extremely hard. There was no goodbye from him to the kids or me—no closure, and that's when it truly hit me. I was silent, and so were they. They were confused, and so was I.

The drive back felt endless. Every mile created a distance I couldn't undo. I gripped the steering wheel, replaying the years of memories—the beginning, the promises, the hope, the trying, and most importantly, their childhood. I kept asking myself if I had done enough, if I had stayed long enough, if leaving meant I had failed. *Did I fail at marriage…did I fail at motherhood…did I fail at enduring the path that the Lord paved for me?*

I've always quoted 1 Peter 5:10 as long as I can remember, always hoping our latter days would be greater. *Did I just forfeit my entire family's Amos 9:13?* I felt weak. I felt stricken. I felt like I had betrayed my husband, my family, and my God. I didn't feel relieved, not one bit. I felt grief layered with responsibility. I felt the weight of choosing something I never wanted. The entire fifteen hours and seventeen minutes felt mundane.

When we arrived in Texas, I sat in the car longer than necessary. The engine was off, but my body was still bracing. I knew that once I stepped out, everything would become real. There would be no going back to the version of life I once knew. That was the moment I understood something painful and honest: Sometimes leaving isn't choosing yourself; sometimes it's admitting there is nothing left to save the way things are. That was when the weight settled: *What now?*

Chapter 6

Monique's Story

"Standing in the Shadow"

I come from a blended family. My mom had six children—three boys and three girls—and only two of us had the same father. My dad also had three children from a previous marriage. Growing up, none of us had the same father, which made for an interesting childhood.

My father was extremely abusive toward my mom—physically and emotionally. I grew up seeing constant fighting, arguments, and few healthy communication patterns. We didn't have much money; we were just above the poverty line. My mom worked constantly, always holding more than one job.

My dad struggled with addiction to hard drugs and alcohol. My mom would say he disappeared all weekend and came home late Sunday night, smelling of alcohol. They fought, and I went to school carrying that weight.

There was a big age gap between my siblings and me: my sister is two and a half years older, my oldest sister is nine years older, and my oldest brother is sixteen years older. Because of these gaps, growing up felt like having second parents in my siblings. They hated my dad. They saw more than I did. He was more violent earlier in their lives, so their perspective of him was very different. As a child, I didn't fully understand that yet. I just knew things felt off.

I remember my mom telling me, "Your dad never knew how to love. His childhood was really bad, and I am trying to teach him how to love." Even as a kid, though, I knew something wasn't right.

I remember being around ten or eleven years old and telling her, "Mom, you can divorce him. I'll be okay." However, she believed in "for better or worse." She loved my dad through everything—until the day he died. I was seventeen then, a high school senior.

One thing about my upbringing is that I was always in church. I tell people I was a "drug baby" because my mom "drug" me to church. The church became our safe haven. We were there almost every day of the week. My mom served in leadership in a traditional Baptist church, and I watched her pray, fight spiritually, and believe that one day my dad would be saved.

Years after my dad passed, my sister found one of those small Bibles where you write your name and the date you gave your life to Christ. My dad had written his name and a salvation date in that Bible. When she told me, we both cried. Based on what I saw growing up, I had convinced myself he was going to hell. But my mother's faith—her consistency—planted something in him.

Still, my experience with my dad was complicated; my feelings did not align with the pain others felt. He was a terrible husband— but a good father to me. He treated my sister and me like princesses. He cooked, he cleaned, he was structured. He never yelled at us or hit us. I didn't even take out the trash until after he died. He would literally plate our food and serve it to us. It felt like he was two completely different people.

As I got older, I learned more about his relationship with his mother—it wasn't healthy. It lacked respect, and I think that carried into how he treated women, especially my mom. Watching all of that shaped me. I made a decision early on: a man would never take advantage of me. I didn't want to be like my mom. In my eyes, she loved too hard. I couldn't understand why she stayed with someone who kept hurting her. So, I hardened my heart in that area. I told myself I would never tolerate that kind of treatment.

My childhood was rough. There's no other way to say it. When my dad died, my siblings had a very different reaction from me. They had seen more of the abuse—things that were hidden from me. My mom had even been seriously harmed by him at one point, something I didn't learn until I was an adult. She had gone to a women's shelter and promised she wouldn't go back—but she did.

By the time I was older, the physical abuse had stopped. It became more emotional—harsh words, lack of love—but not the same level of violence. And because I was the youngest—and honestly, his favorite—I experienced a different version of him. My siblings respected him as my mom's husband, but I don't think his death impacted them the same way it impacted me. As I got older, all of that began to shape how I approached relationships.

My first real experience with love was in high school. I had known this guy since middle school. We went to different high schools, but we stayed connected through mutual friends. We tried dating, but deep down, we both knew we were better as friends. He was supposed to take me to prom, but he cheated on me. So, I took someone else.

I remember running into him at a gas station on the way to prom. All his friends were there, speaking to me, and I completely ignored him. Later, he told me he almost fought my date that night but didn't because he knew I would've hated him forever.

We tried again when we were about nineteen, but it still didn't work. We argued a lot—not physically, but enough to realize we just weren't right for each other. Then, when I was nineteen or twenty, I met another guy. I really cared about him. He had liked me since middle school, but I didn't even realize it at the time. The challenge was—he had a child. At that age, I didn't want to date someone with a kid. But people around me encouraged me to give him a chance because he seemed like a good man.

Then one morning, everything changed. His child's mother called me early in the morning and told me he had been cheating. I confronted him, and I could tell he was lying—he had this habit of stuttering when he lied. I told him, "Let's all meet together and talk about this." He resisted. Then he admitted it had happened "one time." But I knew better. I ended the relationship.

He involved his parents, trying to convince me to stay. His mom told me his dad had cheated on her, and they were still married and happy. Yet I remember thinking, "I don't want that life." I was young, but I was clear. I broke up with him on Thanksgiving Eve. He cried, begged for another chance—but I was done. That was always my pattern. When I saw something, I left.

After college, I moved to Chicago for grad school. During that time, I didn't date much because I was heavily involved in ministry as a youth pastor, wanting to ensure young people around me saw consistency in my life. So, I stayed focused. That focus remained until I met the man who would become my husband, which shifted the direction of my life during that season. I met him in Indiana while visiting a friend. He was a friend of that friend. When I was introduced to him, he said my full name—Monique McCord. I remember looking at him like, *"I don't know you!"*

But he laughed and said, "We're Facebook friends." We had mutual connections, so I didn't think much of it. At the time, I had transitioned out of being a youth pastor and was serving as an executive pastor. We actually had a youth pastor position open at the church, and someone suggested him for it. I told him to send me his résumé.

Months passed, and we ended up giving the position to someone else. Later, he reached out and asked what happened with the job. I told him we had filled it, and he said, "That's okay… we can still be friends." At that point, our friendship began to shift, opening up new possibilities beyond ministry conversations.

We started talking on the phone. At first, it was completely platonic—just conversations about ministry, about what God was doing, about purpose. And we could talk for hours. I remember one day, when I was at the office, he paused in the middle of our conversation.

I asked, "Are you okay?"

And he said, "Man… I think you might be my wife."

I was like—*what?*

We had only been talking for about three or four months. I remember thinking, *"I don't know about this guy!"*

I had never really brought anyone home before. My family had never seen me with a man like that—my brothers used to joke that I was going to be a nun. So, when I finally brought him around, it was a big deal.

Much to my surprise, he fit in perfectly. Especially with my brothers. They're street guys, but he connected with them naturally. And that mattered to me. About a month after meeting my family, he had surgery for kidney cell issues. I remember asking my cousin—who was my roommate at the time—if I should go see him.

She said, "If you were having surgery, do you think he would come?"

I said, "Yes."

She said, "Then you should go."

So, I did.

I stayed that weekend, and it happened to be Mother's Day. His family had this tradition where all the men would cook for the women, and I was there for it. I remember one of his uncles praying, "We're going to pray that God's will be done concerning what we want." And what they wanted…was me in their family.

Months later, on his birthday weekend, he proposed. In front of his family. In front of his friends. And I said, "Yes." We had talked about marriage, but everything happened quickly. We had only been together for about six months before planning to get married the following year.

Then, everything changed. Shortly after getting engaged, I returned from a weekend away—one of the best weekends of my life—and went into a meeting with the elders at the church I'd been part of for over 10 years. They were laying me off. Just like that. Not just me—there were others too—but still. I went from one of the highest moments of my life to having no job.

No stability. No plan. And I didn't do well without stability.

I remember thinking, *"God, what is happening?"* I had given my life to ministry. I had served faithfully. And now everything felt uncertain. But in that space, my fiancé stepped in and said, "I got you." He helped me move into my apartment. I had already committed to the move, but now I had no income, no direction—nothing.

During that time, one of my close ministry friends—the one who eventually married us—said something that stuck with me: "I don't think he's coming home." And one week later…we got married. On a beach in Chicago. No family. No big ceremony. We kept it small because his family lived closer than mine, and we didn't want it to feel uneven.

Looking back…there were red flags. We rushed through premarital counseling. We bypassed important conversations. But at that moment, I just knew—I was going to be a wife.

The beginning of our marriage was hard. I had just lost my job. He had moved to a new city and was trying to find work. He eventually got a job, but it wasn't ideal. We were trying to figure out life together…and I was still grieving. Grieving the loss of my job. Grieving the loss of the life I had built.

I was trying to be happy about being married, but emotionally, I wasn't in a good place. He was trying to create a new normal for us, but I struggled to connect to it. And then I started discovering things about him that I didn't know. Things online. Chat rooms. Conversations. A side of him I had never seen before. I remember thinking: *"Who did I marry?"*

I thought we had been honest with each other. I had shared my truth—my debt, my past, my reality. But now I was realizing…I didn't fully know him. I wasn't sure what to do. Everything in me wanted to run. Because that had been my pattern. But this time, I had said yes to marriage. So I stayed. We got help. We talked through it. We tried to work on it. And the following year, I got pregnant with our daughter.

Now everything felt more serious.

We needed stability.

We needed direction.

We needed something solid.

Eventually, we moved back to his hometown. He felt called to it, and after prayer, I agreed. I told him, "If you get a job with good pay and insurance, I'll take that as confirmation." And he did. So, we moved. We had our daughter. And he stepped deeper into ministry—supporting his spiritual father, who was becoming ill.

There was no clear successor, and eventually the church began seeking leadership. There were multiple candidates. And what followed was one of the hardest seasons of my life. It was brutal. People said things about him. People said things about me. Things I didn't even recognize as true. I was pregnant again. I had a newborn. And we were under constant pressure. Eventually, he was voted in as the senior pastor. And just like that…I became a First Lady with two babies under the age of three, and no idea what that role even meant.

✳ ✳ ✳

Over time, we settled into life. It wasn't perfect, but it was ours. He stepped fully into ministry—what he had always felt called to do. What he had worked toward. And I supported him completely. We moved from helping build someone else's vision into building what we believed God had called *us* to.

We transitioned out of the traditional structure and eventually began our own ministry. And I stood beside him in it. Not because I needed a title, not because I needed a platform—but because I believed in what we were building. At the same time, I was still discovering my own voice again. Ministry for me had shifted. It wasn't just about position anymore—it was about purpose.

And one of the moments that stands out the most in that season was when I hosted a women's conference. It sold out. Every seat was filled. The room was full of women who were hungry for healing, truth, and freedom. I remember standing there, looking out, and realizing that everything I had been through…it was meeting people in real time. Lives were being impacted. Women were being set free. And I could feel it—God was doing something through my story. Through my voice. Through my obedience.

On the outside, it looked like everything was coming together. We had transitioned into full-time ministry. We were building something. We had family, structure, movement, and momentum. It looked like we had found our rhythm. But underneath it all… something was shifting.

One day, I had just come downstairs after taking a nap. I could hear voices raised. That alone was enough to make me pause. Something didn't feel right. So, I walked downstairs. And as soon as I entered the room, I heard her say: "You need to get that girl out of your office."

I froze. Because immediately, I knew this wasn't just a random statement.

So, I asked, "What girl?"

And when she said who it was…my heart dropped. It was our praise and worship leader. Someone I trusted. Someone who was in our space, in our home, in our ministry. Someone I had advocated for. And in that moment, everything started connecting.

The distance.

The shift.

The feeling I couldn't explain.

It all made sense in that one moment.

Chapter 7

Kristina's Story

"Visibly Invisible"

Growing up, I always felt alone. I learned early how to stay to myself, how to shrink quietly into the background. I felt out of place—in my home, in my school, and around my friends and family. Adults would approach my parents and ask, "What's wrong with Kristina? Why is she so serious all the time?" It was unusual for a child to carry so much heaviness so early.

Loneliness felt like not being heard. Loneliness felt like being dismissed. Loneliness felt like watching everyone else have joy and live life while I always carried this heaviness but had no understanding of what it was or where it came from. Loneliness felt like being molested at nine years old and telling a trusted adult, only to have it brushed off as if I was making it up.

Loneliness felt like keeping all my emotions to myself so I would not inconvenience the people around me. Loneliness felt like silencing parts of myself, believing it was easier to become smaller than to be fully seen by someone.

I do not remember much about those early years. I remember always being to myself. I played by myself a lot. I do not know if it was that I did not like other kids, but I never really felt comfortable around them. I was always around people, but still somehow alone. I remember carrying this dark heaviness, but I had no language for it then. People would ask my parents what was wrong with me, and that I needed to smile more, and that I looked too serious. And I think hearing that only pushed me further inward. I was so young, and I did not even know what was going on inside me half the time.

Could it have been the night terrors? The molestation I experienced at the hands of family members? The emotional absence of the people meant to protect me? Or the things I was exposed to far too young? My mother always told me I had night terrors when I was very young. I do not remember those, but I do remember them starting up again after the molestation.

I did not understand what had happened to me in technical terms, but I knew it was wrong. My instinct was immediate. I went straight to a trusted adult because something in me knew what had happened was not okay. But when I spoke up, I was dismissed. After that, I think something in me shifted. Being unheard made me quieter. Being brushed off made me smaller. I learned very early that silence felt safer than vulnerability.

As the middle child, being behind the scenes came naturally to me. My older sibling was experiencing life's firsts. My younger sibling was the baby—needing care, attention, and protection. And then there was I. Somewhere in between.

I learned how to blend into different crowds. I learned how to read rooms. I learned how to become whatever it took to make the people in front of me comfortable. I could mask almost anything without batting an eye. After years of brushing pain under the rug, hiding became instinct. And eventually, hiding became survival. I don't remember much from childhood, but I do have vivid memories of always being at church. Being a pastor's kid meant that church wasn't just something we attended—it was the center of our lives.

Being a pastor's kid meant always being on, always mindful of who was watching. Especially in the Slavic church I grew up in, there were silent expectations placed on us and what felt like no margin for error. Perception was everything, so whatever you were carrying that day, or week had to be left at the door.

We had to appear as if we had it together. Perfect with no flaws. No drama, no pain, no hurt, no sadness could be revealed in the one place people came to lay those things down. I had to act modestly, lest I lead others into temptation. I had to speak carefully, because we were in the house of the Lord and God was watching. With the weight of all those expectations, pretending became second nature. I grew up around God, but I didn't see Him as safe. How could a safe God allow me to experience abuse at such a young age? How could a safe God allow me to attempt to take my life at such a young age? How could a safe God allow me to develop addictions so early? With such a distorted view of people—and more importantly, God—I entered womanhood.

For most of my young adult life, I lived constantly asking why. Why do bad things happen to good people? I believed I was a good person—not because I was whole or honest, but because I hadn't done anything obviously bad. I lived a life of lying, hiding, and overperforming, but I still convinced myself I was good.

Yet, no one really knew who I truly was. I didn't trust people, so I hid everything from them—including myself. My friendships were surface-level. My relationships were placeholders because being with someone—anyone—felt better than being alone with myself.

Even though I was still attending church, serving in ministry, and even working for the church at one point, none of that changed the reality that I didn't truly know God. Not as my Lord, not as my Savior, and certainly not as my Father. I thought that if I kept going through the motions, eventually my heart and mind would catch up. If I did everything right, maybe everything would start making sense.

But the truth remained: I didn't know who I was. And when you don't know who you are, you start looking for yourself in other people. I thought the right job, the right friendships, and eventually marriage would fill the deep emptiness I carried. I knew how to lead. I knew how to serve. I knew how to look like I had everything together.

But the more I tried to fix myself, the more hurt I collected. Part of why marriage seemed so important to me was that somewhere deep inside, I thought it would protect me. Even though I had seen brokenness and dysfunction, I had also seen enough to believe marriage could still mean safety. My parents' relationship, while not perfect, did show me a model of love between a husband and a wife. And I think subconsciously I carried this belief that if I got married, all the bad things would stop happening to me. If I had a husband, I would be protected. If I had a husband, maybe the chaos wouldn't reach me anymore.

Eventually, I thought I had finally found the answer. I was sitting there planning a wedding. At nineteen years old, I believed I had finally made it. I thought this life-altering decision would make everything in my life finally make sense. I believed the person I was about to marry would bring healing, stability, and purpose. What I didn't realize was that the decision to marry hadn't even fully been mine.

We had talked about marriage before. I was nineteen, and he was twenty-four. The relationship had been progressing naturally toward that direction, or at least that's what I believed. But things shifted dramatically when our pastor and the elders of the church found out that we had been intimate.

They gave us an ultimatum. Stop having sex. Or get married. Suddenly, the relationship moved at a pace that neither of us had fully chosen. After he and his parents received my parents' blessing, the wedding planning began quickly.

But just a few weeks later, everything collapsed. He ended the relationship. I felt completely out of control. His family, the church leadership, and the spiritual authority I had been taught to submit to had all been calling the shots. At nineteen, I did not have the maturity to recognize the difference between submission to God and surrendering my voice to people. In my mind, whatever they said was what I needed to do.

When the relationship ended, I was left confused more than anything else. My reality felt warped. I had been gaslit into believing that what had happened had not really happened the way I remembered. Shortly after our relationship ended, he married one of my leaders.

Everything that had defined my identity—my relationship, my church, my community—collapsed all at once. My parents eventually stepped in and confronted the church's leadership. I ended up leaving that church shortly after.

Looking back, I didn't realize how isolated I had been. When the relationship ended, I realized something terrifying: I didn't really have friends. My relationships with family were strained. I had built my entire world around one relationship and one community.

So, I started over with a new job and new friendships, and I moved out of my parents' home. And eventually, I moved halfway across the country. I wish I could say the move was God-ordained and something I prayed about. But honestly, I just wanted to run. I wanted to leave the bad behind and start fresh.

When I first arrived in Dallas, it felt exciting. In my mind, it was a fresh start. I did not know anyone, and that felt freeing. I thought I could become whoever I wanted to be there, without anyone tying me to old versions of myself. Without anyone saying, "Remember when…" I was intentional with my time, with meeting people, and with building something new. I met people almost right away. I went on a few dates. For the first time, I felt like I was experiencing a city, experiencing life, and maybe writing a new story.

When I first got there, I really believed that the move would be my clean slate. That the pain I had experienced would stay behind in the state I left. But only a few months later, reality caught up with me. Everything I had tried to run from had followed me. The cycles. The confusion. The emptiness. Because I had never addressed my past relationship wounds, my patterns simply repeated themselves. Different man. Same story.

I met him in my first week in Dallas, though we did not start dating until a few months later. He had been pursuing me consistently, and, if I am honest, that is what first caught my attention. I had never really been pursued like that before. He was charming. He had charisma. He came off as a gentleman. He took me on extravagant dates, made me breakfast in the morning, and seemed deeply interested in me—my family, my culture, my future.

One of our early dates felt like something out of a movie. He took me to a really nice restaurant in Dallas, then to one of those candlelight orchestra events, and afterward we got ice cream. It felt sweet and thoughtful. He seemed intentional from the start. He would ask me questions about the future, about family, about whether I wanted children, what kind of life I imagined, what kind of life he imagined. It felt like we agreed on so much. Almost too much. That should have been a warning to me.

There was a part of me that felt like it was too good to be true. I noticed how quickly we seemed aligned, how similar our answers were, how easily he became what I wanted to hear. But at the time, it did not register as a danger. It was more like a yellow flag than a red one. I noticed it, but I did not know how to interpret it. I just thought we would see how it went.

The relationship started the way they often do—intense affection, love bombing, promises of forever. For a while, it felt perfect. Until it didn't. He had a temper. He raised his voice a lot, but at first, I did not identify that as abuse. To me, it was just him getting upset and then calming down. I remember one of our first fights. He shut down and kicked me out of his apartment. It felt like whiplash because I still did not understand what I was looking at. One morning, he was telling me to get out, and by that evening, he was buying me flowers and acting as if nothing had happened. That was the first time I really thought something felt off.

But even then, I still had not put two and two together. I think part of that is because I was hardly ever exposed to healthy relationships that taught me how to handle warning signs. I had seen abuse before, so when I started seeing signs in my own relationship, it did not hit me with the force it should have. It was not red in my mind. It was yellow. Familiar. Concerning, but not shocking.

I had also spent so much of my life suppressing things that I had never really learned how to process what I was experiencing in real time. So even when red flags were in front of me, they did not land the way they should have. They felt almost normal.

The abuse started early, but I didn't recognize it immediately. I had been drinking since I was thirteen years old, so my alcohol tolerance had always been high. But after a few months in the relationship, something strange began to happen. Whenever we went out together, I would black out. Completely. I would remember getting dressed to leave the house—and then nothing.

When I woke up the next morning, I would often have bruises on my body. I asked him about them several times. Each time, he had an explanation.

"You probably ran into the kitchen island."

"You must have hit something at the gym."

His explanations filled the gaps my memory couldn't. And his certainty was louder than my confusion. But my body began to sense danger long before my mind did. Eventually, fragments of those nights began coming back to me. Brief flashes of memory that I couldn't fully piece together. Even then, I struggled to trust myself enough to believe what I was remembering.

I wish I could say I left the first time I realized the reality of that relationship. I wish I could say that once I saw it clearly, I walked away. But I didn't. A part of me still did not want to believe it was real. At the forefront of my mind was not my safety, but the fear of what others would think if this were actually reality. How would this reflect on my character? How would this reflect on my family? It felt easier to live in denial than to face the facts in front of me.

As time went on, the reality became harder to ignore. He became more aggressive, and his hatred toward me grew stronger every day. By then, I had developed such an unhealthy bond to him that I did not even know how to begin breaking it. It sounds crazy to say, but he had become like the nucleus in my life. I did not know how to function without the chaos he brought. That chaos had become familiar to my nervous system. Familiar to my mind. And sometimes familiarity feels safer than freedom. So, I made a quiet decision. I stopped drinking when I was with him.

The first time the abuse happened while I was sober, everything became undeniable. What I had suspected all along was finally confirmed. Still, leaving was not immediate. I confronted him about the abuse for the first time. Before that, I had only asked questions when I saw bruises or felt confused. But this time I was direct: this can't keep happening.

It was not a physical altercation that day, but we did have a fight. The next morning, I woke up at three in the morning in excruciating pain. I sat up in my bed, completely disoriented. It took me a few minutes to realize that I could neither hear nor see. It literally felt like my body was shutting down. My nervous system was screaming at me. And this time, I listened. I went to the hospital.

At the hospital, they asked if I was under stress, and I played it off. I said it was just work and stuff because I knew if I told the truth, more questions would come. I did not want to say it out loud—not to them, not to my family, not even to myself in that sterile room under fluorescent lights.

They checked me, gave me medicine, gave me IV fluids, and told me I needed to rest the rest of the week. When I got out, I told him I had been in the hospital. And then he said something that snapped something in me. He almost framed it as if it were my fault that I had ended up there.

That was it.

I did not plan a dramatic exit. I did not tell anyone in advance. It was not some long, drawn-out goodbye. It was a moment. I blocked his number, and when he started blowing up my phone and emailing me, I told him we were done. At the time, he was practically living with me, always staying at my apartment, but during that particular week, he happened to be at his own place. That made it easier. The grace of God was in that detail.

At that moment, I thought ending it would be simpler than it was. What I was not prepared for was what came after. He tried harder to get me back after that than he ever had before. He pushed.

He pursued. And underneath all of that, there was something in me struggling too. The withdrawal was harder than the breakup itself. Because when the chaos left, the silence that followed felt terrifying.

My nervous system had lived in fight-or-flight for so long that peace did not feel peaceful. It felt foreign. It felt scary. And in that silence, I was no longer just confronting the relationship. I was confronting everything that had led me there in the first place.

All the pain.

All the silence.

All the parts of me I had buried.

And suddenly I realized something terrifying: I had run across the country trying to escape pain, only to land in the most dangerous relationship of my life. At that moment, I didn't know how I would ever find my voice again.

Chapter 8

The Story Isn't Always About You

———◆———

"Sometimes you are the star of
a movie that isn't about you."

I heard those words from someone I love and respect deeply, and I have never been the same since. It is a concept that is genuinely hard to sit with—especially as a person of faith. We serve a God who is good. A God who is intentional. A God who numbers our days and knows our names and promises that He works all things together for the good of those who love Him. So, when pain arrives—when the relationship ends, when the diagnosis comes, when the person you trusted betrays you, when the life you built falls apart—the questions that rise up almost involuntarily are: *why? Why me? Why this? Why now?* These questions are not a sign of weak faith. They are signs that you are human.

But there is another question available to us, one that requires a shift in perspective that can only come through a certain kind of maturity—the kind that is forged, not taught. That question is not *why* this happened to me, but *who* might this help someday. That shift changes everything.

* * *

We live in a broken world. Sin entered human existence, and with it came pain—not because God designed it that way, but because we live in the reality of a fallen world, and in that reality, people hurt people. The expression "hurt people, hurt people" is repeated so often that it has almost lost its weight. But the truth inside it is staggering when you sit with it long enough.

In almost every story you have just read in Part One of this book, the pain that was inflicted did not begin with the person who inflicted it. It came from somewhere. It was passed, often unconsciously, from one wound to the next, from one generation to the next, from one broken person to another person who was also trying to survive. The assault that was executed toward these women was almost always the overflow of a pain that had never been addressed, never been healed, never been handed to God. It did not start with the person who hurt them.

And if they are not intentional—if we are not intentional—it will not end with us either. But here is what I believe with everything in me: God did not design the brokenness, but He has absolutely designed a redemption within it. There is something woven into the fabric of human existence—a divine intention—that gives us the opportunity to use what we have survived to reach someone else who is still in the middle of it. Not because the pain was good. But because God is.

* * *

Think about Jesus. He is divine—fully God, the Creator of everything, the one in whom all things hold together. And yet He was wrapped in flesh. He was born into a family, into poverty, into a political climate of fear and occupation. He was misunderstood by the people closest to Him. He was betrayed by a friend. He knew hunger and exhaustion and grief. He wept at a tomb. He sweated drops of blood in a garden the night before His death.

Why? He did not have to experience any of that. He could have redeemed humanity from a distance—but He didn't. He came close. He came all the way down into the experience of being human so that not one of us could ever say He doesn't understand. He is the greatest representation of relatability that has ever existed, God Himself choosing to walk through the human experience so that His comfort would not be theoretical but personal.

That is the model. And I believe He calls us into a version of the same. Not to suffer needlessly—not to stay in pain for pain's sake—but to allow what we have walked through to become a bridge. To let our testimony be the thing that makes someone else feel less alone. To look back at the road we came down and reach back to the person who is still on it.

That is what testimony is. That is what ministry is. They are not two separate things—they are the same thing. Your story, shared honestly, is one of the most powerful forces for healing that exists in this world.

* * *

You have just finished Part One of this book. You have sat with seven women at their most broken. You have witnessed the weight of what they carried—the losses, the betrayals, the choices made from wounds that hadn't yet healed, the seasons that felt like they would never end. It was heavy. It was supposed to be. Because that is what the breaking actually feels like, and these women trusted you with the truth of it.

Before you turn to Part Two, I want to invite you to do something. I want you to shift your lens. Stop asking why these things happened to them. Start asking what God was building through it.

Because Part Two is not just a feel-good ending to a hard story—it is evidence. It is proof that pain does not get the final word. It is seven women standing up after everything, rebuilding with the very hands that were once empty, and discovering that what they survived was always—**always**—bigger than just them.

What you are getting ready to witness is the redeeming power of Christ. Part Two illustrates the determination of women who refused to let their story end at the breaking point: the never-ending love of a mother fighting to heal not just herself but the children watching her. The hope that God still writes beautiful chapters after the ones we were certain were the end. The grace that shows up in the second beginning—the remarriage, the new love, the restored calling, the voice that comes back stronger after it was silenced.

You are getting ready to see what happens when a woman surrenders. When she fights. When she holds on. When she refuses to give up. And when you finish—when you reach the final chapter and understand that you are the eighth woman in this story—I hope you will feel what these seven women felt when they finally understood the purpose behind their pain. Not that it was easy. Not that it didn't cost them everything, but that it was never only about them. It was always, from the very beginning, reaching forward—toward *you*.

PART II
The Rebuilding

The same women. The same stories. What happens next?

Chapter 9

Lauren's Transformation

---◆---

"Love That Heals Instead of Hurts"

We were young, and we were doing it. That was the honest truth of the early days of my marriage to Jason, and I want to give it its due credit before I tell you what it cost. We had an apartment. We also had health and car insurance. We were building something on our own, not on the backs of our parents, not crashing anywhere temporarily. I was working, and he was working as well, and none of it was glamorous, but it was ours. And for a girl who had spent most of her life in instability—in courtrooms and transitions and borrowed seasons of belonging—ours felt like something worth protecting.

We had our son. We started preparing to buy a house. I remember the day I took a pregnancy test after our son's first birthday party, standing there looking at it and feeling devastated in a way I could not explain to anyone around me. We were married. We were doing the right things. There was no reason on paper for the result to feel like a weight rather than a celebration.

But the marriage had already begun its slow disappearance, and I think some part of me knew that adding to it would not save it. What I experienced in that marriage was not cruelty. Jason was never cruel to me. He was a present father—engaged, attentive, genuinely good with our children. What he was not was present for me.

There was a numbness to him that I could never reach through. A distance that existed not just in our intimacy but in our everyday existence—in how we sat in the same room and occupied completely different worlds. I tried everything I knew. I suggested counseling before it was common. I pushed him to explore his family history, believing that if he could find a sense of identity and connection, something in him might open. I prayed over the marriage constantly. I brought him to church week after week, and he came. The atmosphere would move over me in ways I couldn't describe, and I would look over and see that nothing had moved in him at all. I could not understand how the same room could do such different things to two people sitting side by side.

I started beauty school around that time—partly because I thought a second income might take some of the financial pressure off us, and partly, if I'm honest, because staying gone was easier than being home. I would leave at six in the morning and not return until ten at night. I missed my children. But being around them and him simultaneously had become something I couldn't sustain.

At beauty school, a student noticed me. He left notes in my locker. He left flowers. He was attentive in the specific way that someone who is very unhappy at home recognizes immediately—because attention had become the thing, I was most starving for. I kept my distance. I told him I was married, which he already knew. But he could sense what I was carrying, and he knew exactly what to offer.

By the time I stopped keeping my distance, I had already moved into our guest room. I had already told Jason clearly that I wanted a divorce and that he should decide whether to stay in the house while I found somewhere for me and the children to go. I had no intention of making things difficult.

I want to be honest about what that season was—not to assign it a different name, but to give it its real context. I was not swept away by something I didn't choose. I made a decision while in deep pain, from a place of profound exhaustion, because some part of me believed that doing something irreversible would finally give both of us permission to stop. And it did.

* * *

The divorce was peaceful. I know that sounds impossible given everything, but it was. We had built something together—two children, a shared life, mutual respect, even when the love had changed shape. Jason had been a good father. He remained one. We sat across from each other and said goodbye to the version of us that had tried as hard as it knew how, and then we co-parented with a kindness that I think surprised people who knew some of what we had been through.

I did not blame him. That is the truth I want to put on record. Whatever the marriage had or hadn't been, I understood that he was not malicious. He simply was not yet ready for what he had agreed to. And the distance—the numbness, the couch, the walls—was not something he was doing to me intentionally. He was living inside his own unmapped pain. I just couldn't reach him through it, so I eventually had to stop trying.

What I struggled with more than the divorce was the recognition of who I had become inside of it. The version of me that had emerged from years of trying and failing to be enough for someone who could not receive what I was offering was not a version I recognized or liked. The affair, the deliberate unraveling of what remained—none of that looked like the woman I believed myself to be. And understanding the distance between the woman I was and the woman I had become in that marriage became the first real work of my healing.

I threw myself back into ministry. Youth ministry, specifically—being in rooms with young people trying to figure out faith, love, identity, and belonging—was exactly where I needed to be. There is something about pouring into others that keeps you honest about what you yourself still need. I was casually dating. Nothing serious. Moving through life the way you do when you are rebuilding quietly without drawing attention to the construction.

* * *

I had seen him before. When he and his then-wife had attended our church periodically, we had never really connected—we were both part of couples, two lives moving in parallel without intersecting. I knew of him the way you know of someone who exists on the edge of your world without entering it.

Then he came to minister at a ministry event we were hosting. He did a phenomenal job—the kind of job that makes you want to know where that comes from in a person. Afterward, I reached out, just checking in the way you do when someone does something worth acknowledging. I asked how he and his wife were. He told me they were divorced. Had been for a while. I told him the same about Jason and me. Sometime later, he had a ministry event he was planning, so he reached out to coordinate.

I remember calling my aunt to let her know I was going to meet with him, and she said, "Uh-oh," before I could even finish the sentence. I thought, "What do you mean by *uh-oh*?" At the time, I had a boyfriend—nothing particularly serious, but still. I pressed her on what she meant, and she didn't say much. But I think she already knew something I didn't yet. She had some familiarity with who he was, and I think she recognized that two people at the place where both of us were standing, moving in the direction we were both moving—there was significant potential that God was doing something beyond ministry coordination.

We sat across from each other and talked for hours. Ministry. Purpose. Faith. Life. All of it, flowing naturally, one thing leading to the next. And at some point, in that conversation, something shifted—I could feel it even as I couldn't name it. He asked me if I had a boyfriend. I said, "Yes." His next question was: "Is he a man of God?"

I was offended by the question. Not so much that I didn't answer, but enough that I had to sit with why it landed the way it did. Because the honest answer was no. And the honest answer to why that offended me was that somewhere underneath the offense, I already knew it should.

When I got back to my car that night, I sat there for a moment and thought: "*Wow, God. This actually exists.*" A young man who had all the things the world would look at and call attractive—substance, humor, presence, purpose—and who was also genuinely, unmistakably on fire for God. Someone who spent his free time building something for young people, when he could have been doing anything else. I had not been sure that combination existed in a real person I could encounter in real life. And sitting in that car, I felt something I could only describe as hope.

A few months earlier, I had prayed a quiet prayer: "Lord, if this relationship I'm in is not for me, remove it." Within weeks of meeting Brandon, my relationship quietly ended. I did not engineer it. I just stopped fighting what I already knew. When Brandon asked again how things were, I told him we had ended things. And just like that, *we* started.

* * *

I want to be careful here, because the beginning of something God-ordained does not exempt it from being hard. That is one of the most important things I can tell you, and it is something I had to learn in real time. Just because something is from God does not mean it arrives without challenge.

Brandon operated in a deep, real, and complicated fear. He planned to propose more than once and couldn't go through with it. Each time, the fear won. And I—a woman who had spent her entire life managing the emotional distance of people who were present but unavailable—felt the familiar ache of it in a way that was almost unbearable. Because this time it wasn't numbness or indifference. This time it was a man I could see clearly, a man whose heart I understood, a man I genuinely believed was mine. And still the gap.

A woman I trusted, someone who had known Brandon since he was young, came to me during that season and told me plainly: things are all over the place. She encouraged me to seek the Lord seriously—to fast and pray and not move from my own desires or expectations but to genuinely hear His voice and make sure what I had initially felt was real.

So, I did, three days, no talking to anyone. Just me and God. And I prayed the way I hadn't prayed since my grandmother sat across from me with her Bible and asked me if I wanted to be married. Only this time, I wasn't praying from desperation. I wasn't praying for pregnancy or praying under pressure from not knowing what else to do. I was praying from genuine surrender—*Lord, I need to hear Your voice clearly. Not my own feelings confirming themselves. Not my own hope masquerading as revelation. You.*

And I heard Him, not metaphorically, nor as a feeling, I later interpreted. I heard *Him*—tangible and clear—say that Brandon was my husband. And then He said something that stopped me in my tracks. He said that loving Brandon would require me to stretch every capacity I had. That He would love Brandon through me. That I would need to love this man the way God loves—which is to say, without condition, without ultimatum, without the threat of withdrawal as a weapon.

I could never threaten to leave. That was the instruction. And for a woman who had learned from childhood that love was something you performed to keep people from going—and that when they went anyway, you survived by moving on—that instruction went to the deepest part of me and rearranged something.

When I returned to my spiritual advisor and told her what I had heard, she said she had heard the same thing independently. Brandon was my husband. The fear was real, but it was not the final word. We just had to pray against it and walk forward anyway.

So, we did. He proposed, and we eventually got married. And I stepped into what God had assigned me—not as a wife who had finally arrived at the easy part, but as a woman who was about to discover that the real work of her life had just begun.

* * *

What I did not understand when God said He would love Brandon through me is that, for that to be possible, I had to first receive His love myself. You cannot give what you have not received. That truth sounds simple. It is not. Because receiving love—real love, the kind without conditions or performance requirements, the kind that does not require you to manage someone else's comfort or suppress your own needs—was something I had almost no experience with. I had spent my entire life learning how to earn proximity. How to be useful enough, agreeable enough, small enough, brave enough, to keep people in my orbit. I did not know how to simply be loved. I did not know that was even available to me without a cost.

The marriage brought everything back up. All of it. The nine-year-old in the courtroom who yelled her worst memory out loud and was handed nothing but silence after. The girl who wrote a letter for her father's sentencing and learned to put other people's feelings above her own pain. The teenager who gave the last piece of her innocence to someone who was quietly giving the same thing to someone else. The young woman who had prayed for a husband received one, and believed that was the end of the story, not the beginning of a lesson.

All of that was still in me. Layered and buried, and managing itself quietly. And God, through the specific challenges of loving a man who was also being healed, began to surface it all.

There were disappointments in those early years. There were moments when Brandon, carrying everything God was calling him to, did not have the capacity to walk with me through my own healing at the same time. And I would bring that pain to God—not because I had no one else, but because God had specifically instructed me to. He told me early in our marriage that He would heal me Himself so that I could be the rock my husband needed. And so, in the moments when I felt unseen or unmet or lonely in the specific way that marriage can make you lonely, I learned to take it directly to the source.

That is where I learned what receiving love actually means. It means letting God's love toward you be sufficient in the moments when a human being cannot be. It means trusting that you are fully known and fully held, even when the person beside you is in their own becoming. It means understanding that forgiveness is not contingent on apology, and that redemption requires you to place people back in the position they belong in—not erasing what happened, but releasing yourself from the weight of carrying it.

I had to forgive my violator. Not for him—he had long since moved on. For the nine-year-old who had been carrying the weight of his actions in her body for decades. I had to forgive my father for hiring the attorney who cross-examined me, for asking me to write a letter, for being the cool dad when what I needed was the protective one. Not because those things were acceptable, but because I was done being shaped by them.

I had to forgive myself for what I had done inside of a marriage I had prayed into existence. For the ways I had, in my desperation, become someone I didn't recognize. Grace is not a concept I had intellectually doubted—but receiving it personally, for my specific life, in the specific forms my failures had taken—that was different. That required me to believe I was worth it. And that belief had to be built from the ground up.

God did that. Slowly, methodically, through the daily discipline of a marriage that required me to stay when I wanted to run, to speak when I wanted to be silent, to love when I felt empty. He built it.

* * *

Something shifted in Brandon. I cannot tell you exactly when, because it wasn't a single moment—it was more like watching a tide change. The fear that had been so loud in him began to quiet. The commitment that had always been beneath the surface began to rise to the surface. A steadiness emerged that I had not seen before, and what was remarkable about it was that it did not feel like it was coming from him alone. It felt like it was coming through him. Like God was honoring something in the obedience we had both brought to this.

The phrase "beauty for ashes" is one I have known my whole life. But it stopped being a phrase and became a testimony the day

I looked at my marriage—the real, present, daily version—and understood that I was living inside something with no other explanation. I am a woman who was violated at nine years old, who told her testimony in a cold courtroom, and learned to move on. I am a woman who wrote a letter for her father's sentencing, folded the dagger, and kept going. I am a woman who looked for love in every place that was available to her and found, over and over, that proximity is not the same as being chosen. I am a woman who prayed for a marriage that was not the right one, and received it, and had to learn the difference between answered prayer and God's actual will for her life the hard way. And I am a woman who, on the other side of all of it, heard the voice of God clearly enough to obey it—even when the instruction was to stay, to love, to receive, to heal.

* * *

To the one who has been searching for a long time, not just for love, but for something deeper than that: For safety. For belonging. For the feeling of being chosen not because you performed well or made yourself useful, but simply because you exist and you are worth choosing. I know that longing because I have lived inside it for most of my life. I learned early that love came with conditions I had to meet, that people left when you stopped being what they needed, and that the only reliable response to pain was to move forward and not look back too long.

I went through this for you.

For the little girl who had to be brave in a room she never should have been in. Who told the truth out loud and felt the weight of the world's response to it—the questions, the doubt, the burden of having to prove what she knew in her own body had happened. I want you to know that speaking your truth mattered even when it felt like it cost more than it gave. The version of you that walked into that room and said what she knew is the same version that is still standing. She did not break then, and she will not break now.

I went through this for you.

For the girl who learned to put other people's feelings above her own pain. Who wrote the letter, covered the dagger, moved on to the next thing—because that was what surviving required, and she was very, very good at surviving. I want you to know that the ability to keep going is a gift. But it is not a substitute for healing. And one day—when the keeping-going has taken you as far as it can—God will ask you to stop and let Him reach the places that moving forward never touched. Let Him.

I went through this for you.

For the woman who prayed for something and got it, only to discover that getting what you pray for is not always the same as receiving what God planned. I know what it is to take an answered prayer as confirmation—to believe that because something arrived, it must be right. I know what it is to give everything you have to a relationship that was not wrong, but also was not the one. To pray over it, serve beside it, try to love it into what you needed it to be. And I know what it feels like when you finally understand that some lessons can only be learned from the inside of the wrong answer.

I went through this for you.

For the woman who looked at herself in the mirror during the hardest season of her life and did not recognize who was looking back. Who did things she never imagined she was capable of; in the desperation of a pain she could not find another exit from. Who wondered afterward whether grace was available for what she had done—for the specific shape her failures had taken, in the specific context of a life that had been trying so hard and coming up short for so long. Grace is available for all of it. Not as a loophole, but as the very nature of a God who knows every chapter of your story and chose you anyway.

I went through this for you.

For the woman who heard God's voice clearly for the first time, and the instruction was harder than she expected. Who was told to love someone in a way that required every capacity she had—to stay when she wanted to run, to give when she felt empty, to trust when trust had cost her before. I want you to know that obedience to a hard assignment is not weakness; It is the most advanced form of faith. And what God builds in the season of your obedience is something no shortcut could have produced.

I went through this for you.

For the woman who is just now learning what it means to receive love—not to earn it, not to manage it, not to perform for it, but to simply open her hands and let it land. I know how foreign that feels when you have spent your whole life being the one who gives. I know the discomfort of being still long enough to be loved without doing anything to justify it. But I want you to know this: you cannot pour from an empty cup. You cannot give what you have not been given. And the love God wants to extend through you to the people He has placed in your life—your children, your husband, your community, the stranger who will one day pick up a book you wrote—it has to move through you first. Let it.

I went through this for you.

So, you would know that everything had a purpose. The court-room and the dagger and the searching and the wrong marriage and the wilderness season between—none of it was wasted. God does not waste a single thing you have survived. He files it. He tends it. And at the right moment, He reaches back and uses the very thing that hurt you most to heal someone else most deeply.

That is what testimony is.

That is what this book is.

Seven women said yes to telling the truth about what they went through so that you—whoever you are, wherever you are reading this—would not have to face yours alone. And I gathered them because I know what it is to sit in a pain that feels unreachable, and to wonder if anyone has ever been in a room this specific, this dark, this quiet.

Someone has…we all have.

And we went through it for you.

So, when the time comes—and it will come—when God asks you to turn around and reach back for someone who is standing right where you used to stand, I hope you will say yes. I hope you will open your mouth and tell the truth about what it cost, what it built, and what He did in the middle of it. I hope you will hand your story to someone the way these women handed theirs to you.

Because someone behind you is praying for the strength you now carry. And you didn't go through it for nothing. You went through it for them.

With all my love,

Lauren

Chapter 10

Sylvia's Transformation

"Faith in the Waiting"

I relearned how to walk. How to talk. How to dress myself. How to do the ordinary things a body does when it has nearly stopped working entirely. I went through inpatient acute rehabilitation—six hours of therapy a day, six days a week: physical, occupational, speech therapy. The team around me was extraordinary, and I want to say that clearly because I believe God intentionally placed every one of those people in my path. I was a registered nurse. I had great insurance. I had a cousin who knew how to advocate in an emergency room. Every one of those things was grace—not luck, not coincidence, not something I had engineered on my own.

Four months after the stroke, I went back to work as a registered nurse. I want you to sit with that for a moment, because most people do not understand what that means. A major stroke—not a minor one—at twenty-nine years old, and four months later, I was back on the floor as someone who could help bring you back to life if your heart stopped. That is not a normal stroke recovery timeline. That is the faithfulness of God made tangible. For in Him I live and move and have my being—Acts 17:28 stopped being a verse I had memorized and became something I could physically feel with every step I relearned how to take.

But even as my body was recovering, something was shifting in my marriage that I could not yet name. My husband had shown up for me during the stroke and the recovery in ways I had never seen from him before. He was steady. He was attentive. He held things together when I could not. And part of me thought—maybe this is what we needed. Maybe walking through something this serious was going to be the thing that finally brought us into alignment.

Yet, as I returned to myself—as I went back to work, reclaimed my independence, stepped back into the capable version of me that had always led and managed and carried more than her share—a shadow settled over him. His sleep schedule and eating habits changed. The man who had been so present while I was helpless began withdrawing as I became capable again. I had studied him for years. I knew him. And I knew something was deeply wrong, even before I could explain what it was.

What I eventually came to understand was this: the version of our marriage that had existed before the stroke had never been healthy. I had been carrying more than my share—leading, managing, compensating—and I had been vocal about it in ways that did not build him up. Nobody talks about what it means to be the one in the marriage who is always holding things together, and nobody talks about how that dynamic can slowly erode the very foundation you're trying to stand on. We had both failed each other. I had not been the wife who lifted her husband in his weakness. He had not been the husband who initiated, led, and protected. And when the stroke forced a different arrangement—when he had to step up, and I had to receive—something briefly flickered into place. But when I came back, it went out again.

The divorce was finalized two years after the stroke. It was the heaviest grief I had known up to that point—not because it was the loudest, but because it felt like failure in a category I cared about deeply. I had heard the Lord before I married this man. I had felt the inner knowing that I should wait, that this was not quite right, that I was moving ahead of God's timing. And I had moved forward anyway. Now I was standing in the wreckage of a decision I had made with my eyes at least partially open, and I had to figure out how to carry that honestly.

I went back to God's feet. Again. That is what I do. I repented—not just for the marriage, but for the patterns I had brought into it. For the lack of grace, I had shown a husband who was struggling. For choosing good when God had something great waiting. For moving in my own timing one too many times and calling it faith. And then I asked for something I desperately needed: expedited healing. Because I still had a plan. I still wanted to be a mother. And time, at this point, was not standing still.

✳ ✳ ✳

I met my second husband two months after my divorce was final. *Two months.* I know exactly how that sounds, and I understand every raised eyebrow. I was the first person to raise my own eyebrows. I had come out of a stroke, a recovery, and a divorce, and I had been praying since before the divorce papers were signed that God would heal me—not just from the marriage ending, but from everything I had carried into it. I did not want to bring bitterness, resentment, or unresolved wounds into whatever came next. Lord, heal me first. That was the prayer.

And then Jeremy walked into my life, and God said—*now.* I had been at a restaurant not long before, just living my life, when an elderly man walked past my table and said—completely unprompted, to no one in particular except me: "Keep smiling. The Lord sees you."

I didn't know what to do with that at the moment. It was one of those things you tuck away and carry with you because something about it won't let you put it down. I understand it now completely. It was a word for the season I was walking into. Something was coming. And God wanted me to know, before I could see it, that He was already in it.

When I met Jeremy, I asked God one thing: "Show me this man the way You see him." And what I saw was someone I recognized immediately. Not in a swept-off-my-feet romantic way—but in the quiet, settled, inner-knowing way I had been learning to identify as the voice of the Lord. I knew he was my husband. I knew we would have children together. I felt my life getting back on track—not because everything was perfect or resolved, but because for the first time in a long time, I was moving with the guidance of the Holy Spirit instead of running ahead of it.

That didn't mean I made it easy. I want to be honest about that, too. I put that man through an entire emotional marathon before we got to the altar.

He proposed, and I said yes, and two days later I was calling everything into question—

"I can't move to Charlotte,"

"Nobody leaves Texas for a man."

"Are you serious right now?"

"What am I thinking?!"

I took him on a genuine rollercoaster because I was still learning to trust the inner knowing, still working out the difference between godly caution and fear dressed up as wisdom. Yet still, he hung in there. He loved me so steadily and so well through all my uncertainty that it eventually made me grow up in the places I still needed to.

His approach reminded me of something my previous pastor used to say about his wife: "She loved me so well that it made me grow up." I understand that now from the other side of it. When someone extends that kind of grace to you—when they stay when they could leave, when they hold steady when you are spinning—it does something to you. It calls you up—Jeremy called me up.

I left Texas. And it was one of the best decisions I have ever made. We built a life in Charlotte. Ministry together. His three children, who became mine without hesitation—I had always wanted children, and his did not faze me in the least. We built a home, a community, a rhythm that felt like the picture I had carried in my heart since I was nine, when I was playing house in kindergarten. It wasn't perfect. But it was ours. And it was built on the right foundation this time.

* * *

At 37, I became pregnant with our first son. Isaiah Cole. The first trimester was a breeze. I was older, so the genetic testing felt like the responsible choice—I wasn't anxious about it, just thorough. I went in expecting to find out the gender and confirm that everything was developing normally. I anticipated coming home with a gender reveal plan and a name to pray over. Instead, I received a call that brought everything to a halt: "Mrs. Black, the testing has revealed a ninety-six percent chance of Down syndrome."

Everything went still. My first thought—and I mean the very first thought that formed in my mind before anything else—was: there is a four percent chance this test is wrong. And that is more than enough room for God to do what He does best.

I want you to understand what it took to get to a first thought like that. It was not natural optimism. It was not a denial. It was years of learning who God is—years of making wrong turns, coming back to His feet, and watching Him be faithful anyway—that produced a first thought like that. The testing said ninety-six percent. My spirit said four percent is enough.

Isaiah was born on October 11, 2023, at twenty-eight weeks. One pound and six ounces. Preeclampsia had crept in at twenty-six weeks, and after two weeks of hospitalization, he made it clear he was ready to come out and meet us. He arrived early and small and fierce, with a severe heart defect that meant the road ahead was going to be long and hard and full of unknowns. We held on to God. That is all I know how to say about what that season required. We held on.

One hundred and forty-two days. That is how long we had him on this side. One hundred and forty-two days of fighting and praying and showing up at that hospital and watching our son live in a way that had absolutely nothing to do with his size or his diagnosis or the odds that had been stacked against him from before he was born.

The team at Levine Children's Hospital knew our faith from the beginning. They witnessed it up close, day after day. And it did something to them—to the doctors, to the nurses, to the people who cleaned those rooms and changed those linens and passed us in the hallways. People came to us. People asked us questions. People gave their lives to Christ because of what they saw us carry and how they saw us carry it.

His pulmonologist stood in that room near the end and said to us, "I do not know what kind of faith keeps you this strong." But I want to learn about it. What church do you attend?

Isaiah did more in 142 days than most people do in a lifetime, without a single word, without ever leaving that hospital. His fruit remains in every person who watched his parents worship in the middle of the hardest thing they had ever faced and decided they wanted what we had.

On March 1, 2024, Isaiah went home to Jesus. We won. I need you to hear me say that—*we won*. It does not look like winning from the outside. I know that. But eternity is real, and what Isaiah accomplished in one hundred and forty-two days is written there permanently. We won.

* * *

Grief is physical. I need people to know that. It is not just something that happens in your emotions or your thoughts—it lives in your body. After Isaiah, I was recovering on multiple levels simultaneously. My body was still processing what pregnancy, preeclampsia, and loss had done to it. My heart was in a kind of pain that doesn't have clean edges. And my spirit was asking questions I had never had to ask before.

I never asked why. I want to be clear about that. I didn't ask why because I wasn't sure I wanted the answer—or maybe because somewhere deep I knew the answer wouldn't be something I could hold right then. What I asked was, "*How*. How do I carry this? How do I keep going? How do I show up for my husband and his children, for my life, and for my calling when I feel like I have been hollowed out?"

I was armor-bearing for our first lady one evening at a worship night—going because she needed me there, not because I had the emotional energy. I was tired. I was still raw. The room was full of people being healed, delivered, and having breakthrough moments, and I was genuinely grateful for every single one of them. But I was still in the middle of my own grief, and gratitude for others does not make your own pain quiet. And in the middle of that worship, the Lord spoke to me. Simply. Clearly. Four words: "I knew you wouldn't break."

I pushed back. Out loud, in my spirit—I pushed back hard: *"Lord, I am broken. I am in pieces right now. What do you mean you knew I wouldn't break? Look at me. I am shattered."* He didn't say anything else that night. But months later, He came back with the rest of it. I was at work—I was always having these conversations with Him at work, in the in-between moments of the day—and He said: "You understand that you have to partner with me to get things done. I knew you wouldn't break because I knew that, in your weakness, you would always come back to me. You won't stay out there too long. Even in your depression, even in your grief, even in your loss—you will seek me. And that is how I know."

And I was completely undone. Because He was right. I am His most independent, most stubborn, most task-oriented child. I make decisions before I ask. I move before I wait. I have gotten in my own way more times than I can count. But when I am broken—truly broken—I come home. Every single time. I cannot stay out there in my own immaturity and my own lack of understanding and dig the hole so deep that I lose my way back. I always come back. And He was saying: I made you that way. I know you. I planned on that.

Now that I am a parent myself, I understand what He was expressing. Thank God for the children who come back home. The ones who don't stay out there too long. The ones who, even in their worst seasons, turn their face back toward the Father. I am one of those children. And that day, He told me so.

* * *

In May of 2024, I posted something on social media about a joy I couldn't explain. I had no circumstances to justify it. Nothing had been resolved. Nothing had changed. But there was this quiet, certain lightness that settled over me and would not be argued away. I knew it was the Lord. I had felt His presence enough times in my life to recognize when something was coming—when He was moving in a direction I couldn't yet see.

Almost a year to the date of that post, I was pregnant with Kaleb Antonio. This pregnancy was different in every way. Healthy. Strong. The testing came back clear. Everything we monitored showed exactly what we needed to see. We were moving toward a scheduled C-section at thirty-seven weeks, and for the first time in a long time, the future felt like it was expanding rather than closing in.

We were thirty-one weeks—six weeks from our scheduled delivery date—when terrible pain tore through my body in the middle of the night. I knew immediately something was wrong. That kind of pain does not need interpretation. I stayed as calm as I could and told Jeremy to call 911. He moved without hesitation—doing everything that needed to be done, asking nothing of me, anticipating what was needed before I could say it. I felt myself starting to lose consciousness. The last thing I heard before everything went dark was the ambulance arriving, and my last thought was: "*Thank you, God.*"

The last words I processed before I lost consciousness were from a paramedic: "Her pulse is thready, and we're having trouble getting a blood pressure. We need to go now."

A placental abruption. Kaleb had been telling us he was in trouble. He was born at thirty-one weeks, almost five pounds—bigger than we expected, stronger than the numbers suggested. He was gorgeous. He looked exactly like his father. His EEG showed no brain activity, but when the team found a way to bring me to the NICU—still in my ICU bed, still barely recovered from surgery—and laid him on my chest, he opened his eyes. He knew I was there. I know that he knew.

Jeremy held him when they removed the breathing tube. He did not want me to carry that moment—the physical weight of holding our son through that transition. In a situation where neither of us had a blueprint, my husband stood up and said, "I am doing this. You will not have to." And I have never been more grateful for anything in my life. He gave me permission not to be strong. He carried it so that I didn't have to, and in doing so, he gave me something I had needed for a long time—the experience of being covered.

Kaleb Antonio was born on November 23rd. He passed away on November 25th. Forty-eight hours. Two beautiful days. Two sons. Three children total now in heaven, counting the one I had lost in college before I knew how to name what I was losing. And me—still here. Alive in a way that was not guaranteed. Jeremy told me later that the word the medical team kept using while I was in surgery was critical. Nobody could tell him I was going to make it. It could have been two funerals. That is not an exaggeration—that is what my husband was facing while I was unconscious in an operating room.

But I made it. And I am still learning what to do with that.

* * *

I don't have a tidy resolution to offer you. I want to be clear about that, because these stories deserve honesty, and so do you. What I have is this: after Kaleb, I was home recovering from surgery, mentally trying to find solid ground, when a friend—the daughter of our first lady, someone who also does my hair—brought us breakfast. She was in a hurry. She had clients waiting. But she stopped on our porch and said, "Before I leave, the Lord has released me to carry your next baby."

I didn't know what she was talking about. I said, "What do you mean?"

She said, "I had not even told you, but the Lord spoke to me. He told me to start getting my body ready. I have already made an appointment. I am on a weight loss journey. I need to get ready to carry your next child."

She did not know what had happened in that operating room. She did not know the details of my recovery or what the doctors had told us. She just knew what the Lord had said to her, and she was faithful enough to say it out loud on my porch when she was already running late.

I stood there and understood something I needed to understand: He hears us. Even when we cannot form the prayer. Even when the words don't come. Even when all we have is grief and questions and a body that is still healing from the last thing—He hears. The enemy's strategy is suppression. Make her believe it's over. Make her stop asking. Make her too hurt to hope. And God's response was to send someone to my door before I had told anyone what happened, with a word I hadn't asked for and a confirmation I desperately needed.

I reached out around that time to another young woman who had lost her husband while pregnant—one of the only other people I knew who had walked through something of a similar magnitude. I asked her how she planned to move forward. She said, "Sylvia, I don't have a choice. Either I'm going to trust Him, or I'm not. That's all it comes down to."

That is the whole answer. It is not a feeling. It is not a resolved theology. It is a decision you make when you wake up in the morning, and sometimes again before noon, and sometimes again before you close your eyes at night. Every day is a choice. And the alternative—the path that leads away from God when the pain gives you every reason to go—is a darkness I refuse to live in.

I have three beautiful children here on earth. I have a husband who held our son, so I didn't have to. I have a God whose grace and mercy are new every morning, who reminds me that my current troubles cannot compare to what is on the way, who sent an old man in a restaurant to say keep smiling before I even knew what was coming.

I am still asking how. I will not pretend otherwise. I am still in the middle of questions I don't have complete answers to. But I am asking them from a place of faith, not abandonment. I am asking them because I still believe He hears. Because I have seen too much evidence of His faithfulness—in a cousin who asked for a different CT scan, in a hundred and forty-two days of Isaiah's fruit, in a friend on a porch who came to tell me something she had no natural way of knowing—to stop believing now.

He is *still*.

That is my resolution. Not a conclusion—a posture. A daily decision. A choice I make over and over again because I have learned that I am His daughter who always comes home, and that He has always been waiting for me when I do.

He is still. And so am I.

* * *

To *the one who has been praying longer than she expected to.*

The one who had a plan. Who knew exactly how her life was going to go—the order of it, the timeline, the picture—and held onto that plan with everything she had because the plan felt like the one thing she could control in a world that had already asked a lot of her. I understand that grip. I held it too. I made decisions from inside that grip, and I am still learning to carry them honestly. And what I know now is this: God's timing is not an obstacle to your plan. It is the plan. And when we move ahead of it—even by one month, even with the best intentions—we sometimes step out from under a covering we didn't realize we were standing in.

I went through this for you.

For the woman who made a decision alone, in a moment of fear and pressure, and an overwhelming need to protect the future she had worked so hard for. Who carried that decision quietly for years because the weight of it felt too heavy to set down in front of anyone else. I want you to know that what you did in that moment does not determine what God can still do with the rest of your life. Repentance is real. His grace is real. He knew every decision you would ever make before you made it, and He chose you anyway. The plans He has for you were not canceled by your hardest moment. They were waiting for you on the other side of it.

I went through this for you.

For the woman who heard God and moved anyway. Who felt the inner knowing and talked herself out of it because she was tired of waiting, because she had already waited long enough, because surely God understood that. I have been that woman. I took the February appointment when I should have waited for March, and it cost me in ways I carry to this day. But even inside that consequence, God was faithful. He surrounded me with the right cousin, the right moment of advocacy, the right team. His faithfulness is not contingent on our obedience. It is simply who He is. And He is not done with you just because you moved before He said, "Go."

I went through this for you.

For the mother who held her baby and had to let go. Who counted days instead of years? Who has turned down the baby aisle by accident and had to stand there in the middle of a grocery store, holding herself together with both hands. I held two sons. I kissed their feet. I played worship music and told them they did everything right and that they could go. And I want you to know there is no correct way to survive that kind of love. There is only the next breath. And then the one after that. And somehow, mercifully, God provides enough of them.

I went through this for you.

For the woman who is still asking how. Not why—she has made a kind of peace with why, or at least a truce. But how. How do you keep going when the prayers you prayed with your whole heart did not come back the way you asked? How do you call Him faithful when the evidence in front of you looks like loss? I don't have a complete answer. What I have is what a woman who walked it before me said when I asked her the same question: "I don't have a choice, Sylvia. Either I'm going to trust Him, or I'm not." Every day is a decision. Not a feeling. Not a fully resolved theology. Just a choice you make when you wake up, and sometimes again before noon, and sometimes again before you close your eyes.

I went through this for you.

So, you would know that your faith is not naive. It is not the last resort of someone who has exhausted other options. It is the most courageous thing a human being can do—to look at everything that has happened and still say: "He is still good. He is still writing this. He is still for me. And I am not going to let grief steal what God has already promised."

He sees you…Even now…Even in this.

He has not looked away for a single moment at what you have been carrying. And one day—in ways you cannot yet see from where you are standing—it will become clear that He was there in all of it. It was the cousin who asked the right question. In the friend who showed up on the porch. In the old man in the restaurant who said, out of nowhere, to no one but you:

Keep smiling—the Lord sees you.

I went through this for you.

With love,

Sylvia

Chapter 11

Renee's Transformation

◆

"When God Writes a Second Love Story"

I realize now that things were beginning to change before January 2nd. December 18th is when everything shifted—the night before our flight to Colorado, I took a pregnancy test and found out I was pregnant. Corey and I were standing there together when we saw it. We were shocked and so happy. We didn't even know what to do—do we tell people, do we wait? We told a few people right away and waited until Christmas to tell the rest of the family.

The very next morning, we got on a plane to Colorado. That trip looks completely different to me now than it did then. At the time, it was just our first real vacation—the first one we had planned and paid for together as a family. But looking back, I can see it for what it was: God giving us something we didn't know we needed. Something to hold onto.

It was just me, Corey, and the kids. We stayed in a small cabin surrounded by snow—a first for all of us. We slowed down. We were intentional. We played UNO and Skip-Bo, cooked breakfast together, went out in the snow, went sledding and tubing, and even rode horses through the mountains. CJ was three years old, and

Corey and I would just watch him smile at everything and look at each other with tears of joy—because we were so happy to see him that happy. It was the best trip either of us had ever been on.

There wasn't really any alone time for just me and Corey—it was all of us together the whole time. And now I understand why that was exactly right. That was the only time we would all be together like that again. Even then, looking back, there were signs I didn't see clearly at the moment. Corey couldn't participate in everything. The higher-elevation activities—snow tubing—were too much for him. He was dealing with chest pain and just not feeling his best. His doctor had cleared him to travel, but once we got there, you could tell something wasn't right. Still, he did everything he could to be present. To show up fully for all of us. We came home from that trip, and just days later, everything happened.

* * *

And now I was pregnant and grieving at the same time. That combination doesn't have clean edges. I remember asking God: "Why would You give me this baby and take his dad?" CJ was only three years old. I had three children already, all of them grieving. And now I was carrying another one, trying to hold myself together for them while falling apart inside.

At first, I was completely shocked. And then, as reality started to settle, the questions came: Why would you take my husband? Why would you take the man who was my person? Why would you give me a baby just to take his father away?

Grieving while pregnant was one of the hardest things I have ever done. I was trying to process my own pain while also helping my children process theirs. I had to stay strong and calm and stable— for them, and for the baby I was carrying. It was overwhelming, complex, and heavy in a way I still don't have completely clean words for.

And grief, I've learned, doesn't just happen all at once. Cobey is four years old now, and he is just beginning his journey with it. He knows he has a daddy in heaven, but he is still learning what that really means. I can't even tell you when things started to feel normal again. I just know that going back to work in February was the beginning of trying to find some kind of routine. It had only been about six weeks since Corey passed, but the world didn't stop.

That was one of the hardest parts of the grieving process. Your life has come to a complete halt, and everything else just keeps moving. People go to work. Life continues. And you're standing there trying to figure out how to breathe.

* * *

One of the biggest turning points for me was grief counseling. We started going to a place that was primarily geared toward helping children through grief, but they also held a support group for the parents. I started attending those sessions weekly, and that's where I finally felt seen and heard. I was sitting in rooms with other people who understood people who had lost spouses, who were now raising children alone, who were trying to rebuild their lives from something they never expected. Every week, I had to talk about it. Talk about Corey. Talk about what happened. Talk about how I felt. I wasn't avoiding it. I was facing it head-on, week after week. And somehow, that helped.

At the same time, our village showed up in ways I will never forget. People came and stayed with us. They took the kids to school, helped with homework, brought food, helped with bills, gave their time and energy, and resources—whatever we needed. We were carried. We weren't rushed. We weren't judged. We were simply taken care of. And I truly believe that is a huge part of why I was able to keep functioning.

Going back to work was strange. People didn't know what to say, and neither did I. But I showed up. Even when I wasn't fully functioning, I was there. And little by little, I started stepping back into the shape of a normal day.

One of the biggest decisions I made was to sell the house and move. I couldn't stay in that house with everything exactly as it was—I knew that about myself. So I began downsizing, preparing to list it, getting the kids into new schools, and starting our life in a new environment. That process happened alongside months of pregnancy. And then Cobey was born, and that brought another wave of grief all its own. Giving birth without Corey. Having a son without his father. It reopened everything in a new way.

The biggest thing I've learned about grief is this: You cannot fix it. You cannot fill the void. I tried. I tried to fix it for my kids— buying things, creating experiences, taking them places. I tried to fix it for myself—staying busy and distracting myself. But none of it filled the space Corey left. Eventually, I had to stop trying to fix it and start feeling it. We've learned to sit with our emotions, to talk about them, to let them move through us instead of burying them. We've learned that everyone grieves differently and on their own timeline. There's no right way. There's just the process.

* * *

At some point, without even looking for it, my heart was still open to love. Not because I was searching. It wasn't something I set out to do. I knew that I loved being a wife and raising a family. I had experienced a beautiful marriage, and I believed I would want that again someday. But I wasn't on any apps. I wasn't going on dates. It wasn't on my list. And then I met Brandon.

It was completely random. Organic. Unexpectedly. We met at a restaurant, exchanged numbers, and started chatting. In the very beginning, something felt right in a way I recognized—the same quiet, certain feeling I had trusted before. I remember going home and texting my best friend: I'm in love, and I'm going to marry him.

There was no guilt. I want to be clear about that. Because I didn't choose this life. If Corey were still here, we would still be married. So, to me, this was never replacing anything. It was walking in what God had allowed. It was accepting a chapter I hadn't written and hadn't planned.

When I thought about dating again, I knew what mattered most to me. I needed someone who could hold the reality that I would always love Corey. That I would always honor him. That my children and I would always carry him with us—his pictures in our home, his name in our conversations, his family still deeply part of our lives. I needed someone who wouldn't be jealous of that, who could be mature enough to walk with us through the grief instead of around it.

Brandon has done that with so much grace. He has loved us through our grief seasons. He has embraced Corey's family as his own—spending holidays with them, building a relationship with them, and honoring what Corey meant to us. He has created space for us to remember, to cry, to celebrate. He has been part of God's redemption in our story in a way I couldn't have designed or asked for. God gave me beauty for ashes. Exactly what He said He would.

* * *

Now I live in a place where both joy and pain coexist. And I've learned that that's okay. That they can coexist. Honoring one doesn't negate the other. We still talk about Corey. We still cry. We still mark the days that matter—his birthday, the anniversary of his passing, the moments when one of the kids says something that sounds exactly like him. We still honor him, and we always will. And at the same time, we laugh. We love. We build. We live. The joy and pain are real. Both exist. And both are part of our story.

If I had to say one thing to someone walking through something like this, it would be this: You will be okay. Not because it won't hurt. Not because it won't be hard. But because God will sustain you in ways you can't see yet from where you're standing. I have been through so much—loss, grief, forced independence, growing up too fast, rebuilding again and again. And every time, I have made it to the other side.

I worshipped my way through. I cried out to God every day, put my heart in a posture of surrender, and let Him carry what I couldn't. I never found myself angry at Him—curious about the why, yes, but never angry. And I believe that is what made the difference. Not that I had everything figured out. But I kept bringing what I had to Him, even when what I had was just tears.

* * *

To the girl who grew up independent before she was ready to be.

The one who figured things out on her own, not because she wanted to, but because that was the only option available to her. Who became resourceful and strong and capable long before anyone should have had to be—and who spent years mistaking that strength for wholeness, not realizing she had skipped over the part where someone was supposed to show her what love and stability actually looked like up close. You learned how to survive, and that mattered. But surviving and thriving are two different things, and it took a while to learn the difference.

I went through this for you.

For the girl who found herself in situations she was never prepared for—loving people who were undeserving, knowing better, and staying anyway. The girl who was looking for something that felt like family, even when it kept falling apart. The girl who made decisions with the information she had, in the circumstances she was in, before anyone had given her a roadmap for any of it. I want you to know that those decisions are the beginning of a story. Not the end of one.

I went through this for you.

For the woman who finally found something steady. Something safe. Something that felt like it could actually last—and then had it taken from her in a single night. Who stood in a hospital room and heard two words that split her life into before and after. Who drove home to children who were grieving while carrying a baby, trying to figure out how to keep standing when the ground had completely disappeared. I know what it's like to ask God why He would give you something so beautiful and take it so soon. I know what it's like to have no answer and have to keep going anyway.

I went through this for you.

For the woman who tried to fix grief and couldn't. Who bought things and planned things and stayed busy and distracted herself and coped in every way she knew how—and still woke up every morning to the same silence, the same empty space, the same undeniable truth that you cannot fill what love left behind. The moment you stopped trying to fix it and started allowing yourself to feel it—that was not giving up. That was the bravest thing you did. Grief is not something you solve. It is something you carry, learn to carry differently, and eventually learn to carry alongside joy.

I went through this for you.

For the woman who felt guilty the first time she laughed again. The first time her heart opened when she was certain it never could. The first time she met someone and felt something real, she immediately wondered if feeling it meant she had betrayed the love she still carried. You have not betrayed anything. Grief and love can live in the same heart at the same time. The love you had does not disappear—it becomes part of you. And finding love again does not replace what you lost. It proves that your heart is still alive.

I went through this for you.

So, you would know that you will be okay. Not because it won't hurt. Not because it won't be hard. But because God will sustain you in ways you cannot yet see from where you are standing. There will be days you don't think you can stand, and somehow you will. There will be nights that feel endless, and somehow morning will come. There will be a moment—unexpected, unasked for—when joy finds you again. And when it does, you do not have to apologize for it. You do not have to earn it. You just have to receive it.

I went through this for you.

So, you would not feel as alone as I did. So, you would know that, even after everything breaks, you can still choose to live. That you can honor what you lost and still build something new. That the story God is writing through your life is not finished—not even close. And one day, without asking permission, without betraying the love you carry, you will feel joy again. That I can promise you.

With love,

Renee

Nakeisha's Transformation

"Rising from the Ashes"

After my son was born, I tried to keep everything going at once. Academically, I was still strong—school had always come naturally to me, and that hadn't changed. I was even on the cheerleading team for a while, trying to hold onto some version of a normal high school experience. But the reality of being a fifteen-year-old mother living in someone else's home meant that my availability was always conditional on what was happening around me.

When Cynthia and Weldon had something going on, and there was no one available to watch the baby, I stayed home. Games got missed. Events got missed. Cheerleading eventually became impossible to keep up with.

Academically, I held on longer than I did to anything else. That part of me was stubborn about quitting. But by my junior year, even school had to go. Not all at once—I went the first week or two of that year, tried to hold the pieces together one more time. But after that, I stopped going so I could work more hours, bring in more money, and actually take care of my son the way I needed to.

Even though Cynthia and Weldon had opened their home to us, I was not built to be a guest without contributing. That was not something anyone told me—it came from inside me. They had their own children, their own finances, their own responsibilities. I had a baby, and I had myself, and I was not going to let someone else carry the weight of that indefinitely. I received government assistance for a period of time, and I am not ashamed of that—I used every resource available to me because that is what survival requires. But I also worked. I also contributed to the household. I also made sure I was doing my part, because waiting for someone else to do it for me was not a mode I had ever been able to afford.

* * *

When my son was around a year old, I started moving toward getting out on my own. One of Aunt Tanya's sisters—we called her Fat Baby, her real name was Sarita—told me about a women's shelter that could fast-track me into housing. The strategy was simple: move into the shelter, sign up for everything, and get pushed to the top of the list. I didn't love the idea of a shelter. But I understood the math. So my son and I packed what we had and moved in.

I did not plan to stay long. From the moment I walked through those doors, I signed up for every program available—housing assistance, section eight, anything related to getting into a permanent place. The shelter had a childcare arrangement with a daycare that would come get the kids during the day, which meant I could work a shift and attend GED classes in the evenings without losing care for my son. I moved through every requirement as fast as I possibly could.

Within about two weeks, I had completed everything I needed to take the GED exam. The program was through Dallas Can Academy, which worked directly with the shelter. I went in, did the prerequisites, took the test, and passed it. They held a graduation—blue cap and gown, a small stage, you walked across, and they handed you your diploma. It was plain and simple, and it was *everything.*

I hadn't finished high school the way I was supposed to. I didn't get to experience a traditional senior year. I didn't go to prom, order a class ring, or walk across a stage with the people I had grown up with. None of that happened. So when I crossed that stage at Dallas Can Academy with a cap on my head that was probably a little too big, that was my graduation. That moment belonged to me. I had earned it in ways most people who earn a diploma never have to.

Not long after, housing came through. At seventeen years old, I moved into my first apartment. There was no furniture shopping trip; no putting things together the way you see it done. There was a mattress on the floor, and a few dishes accumulated slowly. I built up from nothing, one small thing at a time. Yet, the space was ours. Mine and my son's. Our own place. And that mattered in a way I don't have perfectly clean words for. After years of rotating through spaces that belonged to other people, we had somewhere that was just ours.

* * *

Around the time I was getting settled into that apartment, I met Antoine. I met him through my cousin Komeka, who was one of Aunt Tanya's nieces and one of my closest friends at the time. She was seeing Antoine's best friend Tony, and the four of us ended up in each other's lives constantly—best friends spending time with best friends, the way those things happen naturally when you're young. That's how Antoine came into my orbit.

What I didn't expect was how steady he was about it all. He wasn't deterred by the fact that I was a young mother. He wasn't put off by my circumstances or embarrassed by where I was in life. When I moved into the shelter before getting my apartment, he still came and picked us up, took us places, dropped us back off at the end of the night without making me feel like any of it was unusual or beneath him. That kind of consistency—showing up without making you feel like a burden—was not something I had experienced often. It meant something to me.

He eventually moved into the apartment with us. And what we built in that season felt real. He used to write me love letters—actual handwritten letters, the kind that people don't write anymore. He proposed to me. We were serious in the way young people can be serious when they genuinely care about each other and are trying to build something out of very little. For a season, it genuinely felt like we were making a family and a future together. And then I got pregnant *again*.

The second pregnancy was completely different from the first in every way that mattered emotionally. I didn't have to hide it. I wasn't scared of getting caught. We were excited. We were actually trying for a baby—a planned child, something I hadn't experienced before. We had two incomes. We had an apartment. We were moving forward. I was not a frightened freshman hiding a pregnancy from the world. I was a young woman building a life with a partner who wanted to build it with me. That feeling—of being chosen, of being planned for, of a pregnancy that was wanted—was something I had never had before. I held onto it.

* * *

I don't know exactly what shifted or when. There was no big blowup I can point to. Not a single conversation that I can trace back to the moment things went wrong. We were fine, and then somewhere in the middle of the pregnancy, we weren't together anymore. He started seeing someone else. I was still carrying his child, still in the relationship I thought we were building, and by the time I understood what was happening, it had already happened.

I went through most of that pregnancy without him. No calls. No checking in. Just me, growing larger, working, getting through each day with my older son, a baby on the way, and a relationship that had dissolved without giving me any real warning.

When it came time to deliver—via C-section—I already knew not to expect much. I was prepared for him not to show up. What I was not prepared for was what actually happened. He showed up at the hospital. He brought her with him.

I was lying in a hospital bed. I had just had surgery. I was holding our newborn son for the first time, still in the physical aftermath of a C-section, still in the thick of everything that comes with bringing a child into the world, when he walked through the door with another woman beside him.

His mother was furious. His sister was furious. They could not understand why he would think that was acceptable—why he would choose that moment, of all moments, to make that statement. And I couldn't either. He didn't have to bring her. Even if he was seeing someone else. Even if our relationship was over. I believed there was a time and a place for that introduction. The hospital room where the mother of your child was recovering from surgery, while simultaneously meeting your newborn son for the first time, was not it.

Yet, I couldn't say any of that the way part of me wanted to. I had just been cut open. I was physically unable to respond the way the situation deserved. I had to lie there and manage the emotions and the shock and the humiliation on top of everything else my body was already trying to manage, completely helpless to do anything about what was happening in that room. I held my son, I stayed still, and I got through it. Because that is what I had always done.

* * *

After the hospital, I couldn't go straight home. The C-section had left me with an open wound that needed real nursing care. I had to go stay with my Aunt Mushie so she could help me heal. My body needed someone to look after it, and I needed to let someone do that, which was not easy for me. Once I was physically able again, I moved to Pleasant Grove to be closer to her so that I wouldn't be in North Dallas alone with two kids and a body still putting itself back together.

Antoine stayed in the picture for his children. Whatever happened between us, he never made his sons pay for it. He showed up for both of them—my older son included, treating him no differently than his own. That matters, and I want to say so clearly, because it matters to a child to have a man show up for them consistently, and he did that.

But romantically, things between us were never steady again. We went back and forth, the way people do when there's history, children, and unresolved feelings all tangled together. Together and not together. In and out. At one point, we went through the entire process of buying a house—got all the way to the end of it—and at the last minute, he backed out. I moved forward anyway. That is the only direction I have ever known how to move.

My Aunt Mushie and I went into that house together. My brother eventually came to stay there too. That house became something that none of our individual circumstances had pointed toward—it became a place with roots. People gathered there. Life happened there. It was the first place that felt like something I had made rather than something I had survived.

* * *

Around that time, I also entered the corporate world. The job I landed was in downtown Dallas, and El Centro College was nearby. The company offered tuition reimbursement for classes, so I could take courses right after my shift without having to pay for them separately. So that became my life: work, class, and home. That was it. I didn't have a social life to speak of, and I wasn't looking for one. I had two kids. Being out there was not an option I had the bandwidth for. I kept my head down and focused.

My relationship with the church during those years was honest—which is to say, inconsistent. I had grown up at Prayer of Faith. I had sung in the choir, been there multiple days a week, done all the things. But once I was an adult managing everything alone, that consistency fell away. I wasn't angry at God. It wasn't a decision I made consciously. I just didn't know how to build a personal relationship with Him, since I had only ever understood church as a place you went because someone made you. My mom had dragged us every Sunday without coming herself. And now that I was on my own, I didn't know how to make faith something that belonged to me rather than something I had inherited.

So I went when I went. Sometimes on Sundays. Sometimes not even that. The people I loved were still there, and they never pressured me. They knew what my life looked like. They gave me room to find my own way back, and that grace meant more than any amount of showing up required.

What got me out of bed every day wasn't church attendance. It wasn't inspiration or motivation in the way people talk about those things. It was simpler and more concrete than that. It was my kids. I did not want them to see me quit. I had been given so many reasons to stop: abandonment, teen pregnancy, dropping out, a relationship that fell apart while I was pregnant, and a body that had been through two deliveries before I was twenty. Any one of those things could have been the moment someone decided they had been through enough and sat down. I didn't sit down. Not because I was extraordinary, but because I looked at those boys and understood that what I did next was something they were going to carry with them. I wanted them to carry a mother who kept going.

So I kept going. I started with the associate's degree, and I walked across that stage like it was the most important moment of my life—because in a lot of ways it was. I hadn't walked across a stage with my high school class. I hadn't gotten a graduation ceremony, a cap that fit, a party, or any of it. The associate's degree was my high school graduation, my college graduation, and my proof all wrapped into one. Every degree I earned after that, I walked across a stage for, because every single one of those moments was one that the circumstances of my early life had tried to make impossible.

My brother started calling me a professional student. He wasn't wrong. I kept going back because every time I came out the other side of something, I understood a little more clearly that my beginning was not my destination.

* * *

My mother came back into our lives somewhere along the way, though I couldn't give you an exact year or tell you how it started. We always knew she was somewhere in the old neighborhood. We had known that for years. I never went looking for her—I had learned a long time ago not to need things that might not show up.

But at some point, she started appearing again. Word reached her that I had children, and she began coming around to see us. Sometimes she would stay for a while. Sometimes she would help with household chores. She wanted to try to be present, and I believe that wanting was real.

But addiction is still addiction even when someone wants to do better. When she was having a good stretch, those visits felt like getting pieces of my mom back—the version of her I had been missing since I was thirteen years old, sitting in a dark apartment. When she wasn't doing well, it felt like caring for another child. You never knew which version would walk through the door. And underneath every visit, in the back of my mind, was the question I had been living with since the lights first went off in that apartment: *How long is she going to stay this time?*

I never stopped loving her. I want to be clear about that. But loving someone and trusting them are different things, and the distance between them is where I had been living most of my life.

*   *   *

When I look back at everything I have walked through, I don't see a story about surviving; I see a story about building. There are so many things that could have broken me, and didn't. Abandonment at thirteen. A pregnancy I hid for seven and a half months alone. Dropping out of high school. A relationship that ended in a hospital room while I was recovering from surgery. Two kids before I was twenty. A mother who kept leaving. None of it was the end.

If I could sit across from a fifteen-year-old girl who is pregnant, scared, and doesn't know where her mother is, I would tell her this: whatever decision you make about your pregnancy, you will be okay. Whether you choose adoption, abortion, or to raise your child yourself, life will keep moving forward. You can build something from very little. You can become stronger than the place you started.

Your life does not end at your hardest moment. Sometimes that moment is just the opening page of the story God is writing through you. I didn't go through all of this for nothing. I went through it for you.

* * *

To the one who grew up faster than you should have. The one who came home to find the lights off and a parent who was supposed to be there, but wasn't. The one who learned to hold things together with nothing—no money, no guidance, no one telling you what to do next. I know what it is to be a child carrying adult weight with no language for how heavy it is. I know what it is to protect the very person who left you, to stay silent about your own pain because you didn't want to get anyone in trouble. I know what it is to sit in the dark with a little brother and figure out how to make it to the next day.

I went through this for you.

So you would know that being left behind does not make you unlovable. The abandonment was not your fault. You were a child, and you deserved to be protected. And even though no one protected you the way they should have, what that season was doing inside of you was building something you couldn't see yet. It was building the woman who would refuse to stop. The woman who would show up for her children, the way no one had for her. The woman who would keep going even when keeping going made no sense.

I went through this for you.

For the girl who found out she was pregnant and her first thought was I'm going to get in trouble—and then realized there was no one left to get in trouble with. For the girl who had adults making decisions about her life around her as if her voice didn't count. I want you to know what someone told me when she pulled me aside at my own baby shower: "You don't have to do this if you don't want to. Nobody can force you. Your voice matters. It always has. Don't let anyone plan your life without your permission—no matter how young you are, no matter how alone you feel."

I went through this for you.

For the woman who loved someone and built something real with him—and then watched it fall apart in the most humiliating way possible. Lying in a hospital bed, recovering from surgery, holding your newborn son, while the person who should have been standing beside you chose to be somewhere else entirely. I know that particular kind of hurt. The kind that doesn't just break your heart but breaks your dignity. But that hospital room was not the end of your story. That moment only determined that this particular person was not the one who would walk with you into everything that was still coming. And so much was still coming.

I went through this for you.

So, you would know that your beginning is not your destination. I know this because I was you. I know this because I held that positive pregnancy test alone. Because I moved into my first apartment at seventeen with a baby and a mattress on the floor and signed up for every program I could find—not because I had it figured out, but because I refused to stay still. I know this because I walked across a graduation stage for my associate's degree and felt something shift inside of me. A quiet, certain knowing that where I started was not where I was going to finish.

Whatever hard moment you are in right now—whether you are fifteen and scared, or starting over with nothing, or sitting somewhere wondering how you got here—it is not the end. God is not finished writing your story. The chapter you are in right now is not the one that defines you. The one that defines you is still being written. Keep going.

I went through this for you.

With love,

Nakeisha

Chapter 13

Chas' Transformation

"Grace for the Second Beginning"

Divorce doesn't end a story the way people think it does. There's no dramatic release. No sudden lightness. No moment where everything finally makes sense. What comes instead is silence—thick, unfamiliar silence—and the slow realization that survival, which had once been shared, now belongs to you alone.

What surprised me most wasn't the loneliness. It was the weight. For years, Ken had been the provider in certain ways. I had run the home, carried the emotional labor, held the schedules, and tended to the children's needs. But I had never carried the full financial and practical weight of a household completely alone. After the divorce, that shifted overnight.

There were moments I would sit by myself and realize how unprepared I felt—not because I was incapable, but because I had never had to trust only myself before. Strength had always been shared, even when the marriage was broken.

Now, there was no one to defer to. Every bill, decision, and consequence rested on me. Our children's future depended on my choices, and the weight was heavier than I expected. I grieved not just the marriage, but also the safety and structure I'd taken for granted.

Motherhood doesn't pause for heartbreak. Bills don't wait for healing. Life kept moving, and I had to move with it—even when I felt completely unprepared. I worked. I scrambled. I learned quickly what I didn't know. There were moments I was proud of myself—and moments I was terrified. I didn't have the luxury of collapsing, even when my heart felt shattered.

Moving back to Texas was easier than I expected, only because I had a small village still there—people who helped me find a place, helped me settle in, helped me breathe. The familiar streets helped too. But what wasn't easy was watching Mackenzie start high school in a city full of strangers. She had lived through the instability of our marriage. She'd already learned not to get too comfortable anywhere. And here we were again—new city, new school, starting over.

I knew that feeling in my bones.

* * *

In the middle of rebuilding, I found myself in another relationship. He was someone from a family I'd known years before. A good man. A great heart. He stepped in and started helping with the kids' school runs, homework, and dinner, while I was working 12-hour shifts as a director. I told myself I was grateful. I told myself this was what healthy looked like.

But if I'm honest, I was in a very vulnerable place, and I didn't know it yet.

I had never truly been alone. Not really. I went from Cannell to Ken to marriage without a real season of just being with myself, learning myself, trusting myself. So, when someone showed up and started filling the space, I confused relief for love.

The red flags were there. I looked past every one of them because my hands were full and I needed help. He was a mama's boy in the way that meant his mother and his family made decisions he should have been making. When things came up—things I needed him to protect my children from, things I needed him to address—he was too afraid of his own family to stand up. And for a woman who had spent her whole life needing to feel safe, that was a dealbreaker I couldn't explain away. It took two and a half years. But I ended it.

The hardest part about leaving wasn't leaving him—it was admitting that I had done it again. That I had stayed longer than I should have. That I had let something not right become familiar because familiar was easier to manage than being alone.

After therapy—real therapy—I started to see the pattern clearly. I was so afraid of abandonment that I would accept the wrong things to avoid being left alone. I had even taught Ken, in the early years, to treat me the way he did—not because I deserved it, but because I kept showing him that people pleasing was the price of my presence. When he didn't treat me right, I blamed him. But I had built the conditions. I had never stood on business. I had never said: "If you leave, then you leave."

That realization cracked me open in a way grief hadn't. Grief is something that happens to you. This was something I had to own.

* * *

Ken never fully disappeared. He was always somewhere nearby— for the kids, for co-parenting, for the logistics of raising children together after a divorce. We would coordinate pickups. We would end up at the same events. And somewhere in all of that necessary proximity, we started actually talking.

Not performing. Not managing. Talking. We had never really done that when we were married. He was in the military. I was in ministry, motherhood, and survival mode. There was no space for friendship. But now, sitting in parking lots while the kids played, going on co-parenting outings, we had no choice but to be in the same space with nothing urgent between us. So, we talked.

I started apologizing—not for the marriage ending, but for what I hadn't seen clearly before. After therapy, I realized that I had expected him to be something for me that I had never been for him. I had never once stopped to ask how he was doing. I had been so busy protecting myself that I had neglected to see him. And I told him that.

He listened. And we kept talking. One day, driving home after one of those long conversations, I told him something I had said to him in the early years as a disclaimer: "I used to always remind you that I loved you, but I wasn't in love with you." And I said: "I can honestly say now that I think I'm falling in love with you."

He was quiet for a moment.

And then he said, "You've always been my person."

That was the confirmation we needed. But knowing it and being willing to risk it were two different things. We had already destroyed what we'd built once. Both of us carried the memory of what that had cost—the children who absorbed it, the years we couldn't get back, the version of ourselves we'd had to bury in order to survive the divorce. Loving him again didn't feel like a victory.

It felt like standing at the edge of something I was terrified to fall into again. We moved slowly. More honestly than we had ever moved before. We talked about what we had done wrong. We talked about what we needed. We stopped trying to be the version of ourselves that performed well and started being the version that was actually true.

For a season, we were together without being married. We were okay with that. We both knew we had failed, and neither of us wanted to run toward another commitment without being sure of what we were building.

* * *

Then we came to church. Ken came back to God before I did. I watched from a distance first. I wasn't angry at God—I was guarded. I had been away from church for seven years, and part of me felt like I had been gone too long to return without consequence. Like I had made too many wrong turns to walk back through the doors, as if nothing had happened. What I eventually understood was that I wasn't resisting faith. I was resisting exposure. Because coming back to God meant letting Him into the places, I had worked very hard to manage on my own. My independence had become a wall. And I had mistaken the wall for strength.

But God is patient. He didn't rush me or shame me. He waited. And exhaustion finally did what resistance couldn't—I got tired of carrying everything by myself. Tired of half-alignment. Tired of calling control by the name of strength.

We attended church together, and it was our son who led us to the altar. Standing there, I didn't feel excited. I felt convicted. Seven years had gone by. I knew better. I had always known better. That altar moment wasn't fireworks. It was sobriety. Conviction has a way of removing your excuses without raising its voice. I wasn't crushed by guilt—I was grounded by clarity. For the first time in a long time, I could see the difference between surviving with God somewhere nearby and actually living with Him at the center.

From that point, alignment stopped being a concept and became a decision. Our church leaders encouraged us to seek God about remarriage—not comfort, not convenience, but God. And God was clear.

When I brought it up to Ken, I braced for resistance. I remembered the tension that had come before every prior conversation about commitment. But this time he said, "Let's go. Let's do it." The only thing he asked was that we do it our way. Small. Ours. Not for anyone else.

I responded, "I'm in agreement."

Not long after that, we got our marriage license and talked to our pastor. The following week, we were married.

This time, while riding to the courthouse, I felt my heart racing. Not from fear of him. From the weight of finally marrying someone I actually, fully, with my whole self, loved. I had never felt that before. Not like that. Not all the way through.

We were in the room beforehand, texting each other: "Are we really doing this? Why are we sweating? We're nervous for what?" And that nervousness—that's how we knew. That's how a wedding is supposed to feel, even when no one's watching.

When he stood up and gave his vows from the top of his heart, unrehearsed, just truth—I was done. I was completely undone. God didn't restore what we had. He rebuilt what we never learned how to build the first time.

This marriage is different—not because we are flawless, but because we are submitted. God is no longer an accessory to our relationship. He is the foundation, the filter, and the authority.

We don't have a perfect story. We have an honest one. And peace—the kind I had been searching for in every house, every city, every relationship since I was a little girl rotating through summers, I didn't ask for—that peace came. Not all at once. But it came. And it stayed.

* * *

To the person reading this in the middle of your own wreckage—after a marriage that didn't survive, after a relationship that looked like a rescue and turned into another lesson, after you've asked God why He would let you want something so badly and still let it fall apart—I need you to hear this:

You are not too far gone.

I know what it feels like to carry wounds from childhood into every room you enter. I know what it feels like to confuse safety with proximity, and to stay long after you should have left because leaving felt like one more person walking out the door. I know what it feels like to rebuild your life from nothing, with children watching, and no guarantee that anything you're building will hold.

I went through this for you.

So that you could see what healing in pieces actually looks like. Not one clean moment of breakthrough—but therapy, and silence, and hard conversations, and praying on the floor of a closet, and driving sixteen hours not knowing what was on the other side. Healing is rarely beautiful while you're in it.

I went through this for you.

So that you would know that your pattern is not your destiny. The things you learned to do to survive—the people-pleasing, the shrinking, the staying too long—those things kept you alive when you needed them to. But you don't have to keep living there. You can unlearn what fear taught you. You really can.

I went through this for you.

So that you could see that sometimes God allows restoration—not because you deserve an easy ending, but because He is still working. He didn't restore what Ken and I had. He rebuilt something we never had the tools to build the first time. And that difference matters.

Restoration isn't returning to what was broken. It's being given the wisdom and the foundation to build something that can actually hold.

If you are standing at the edge of a decision, you're afraid to make—whether it's walking away, or walking toward, or finally walking into a church you've been avoiding for seven years—He is not afraid of your hesitation. He is not offended by your questions. He is patient in ways that will undo you, if you let Him. I am living proof.

Whatever you went through, whatever you're still in—it is not the end of your story. And one day, if you're willing, it will become the very thing that saves someone else.

With love,

Chas

Chapter 14

Monique's Transformation

"When God Restores Your Voice"

When everything came out, I was completely shocked. This wasn't just someone random—this was someone who called me "sister." Her children called me "TT." Her youngest even had my middle name. I had been in the hospital when she gave birth. We did life together. Ministry together. Family *together*. I was trying to make sense of what didn't.

I'm a person who believes in conversations. If there's an issue, we talk about it. So I needed answers. We went quiet for a little while, and then I said, "We need counseling. We need to figure out what this is."

He denied any physical relationship. He said it wasn't sexual— just emotional. That they had shared too much about their personal lives. Still, I needed more answers. I scheduled a time and met with her at a Starbucks. I did not hold back. I asked questions. I pressed. I needed clarity. She cried and said she was sorry, but she insisted nothing physical had happened.

At the same time, we learned another piece that shifted everything: her husband revealed they were already going through a divorce, something my husband and I didn't know because they had filed in a different county. Now, it felt like everything started to unravel at once.

We had to tell her husband what had been said. He was furious. He felt betrayed—not just as a husband, but as a friend. At that point, he questioned whether it had gone beyond emotions. But just as all of this chaos unfolded, it grew even more complicated: we were all still attending church together. He was still playing. She was still leading worship. And we were all still showing up in the same space—trying to act like something hadn't just broken.

Meanwhile, my husband and I were in counseling, and the counselor told us plainly: "You're at a crossroads. You either fix this, or you don't." Our daughters were young—seven and eight—and I knew whatever decision we made would impact them deeply. But that wasn't the only pressure. The church we had merged with was now turning on him. The man we partnered with started questioning his leadership—saying, "We're paying him all this money, and the church isn't better." He even asked me, "So what does he do at home?"

And I told the truth. I said, "He doesn't really do much. I'm here. His mom is here. He takes out the trash, mows the lawn, picks up the girls…" And that honesty created tension.

First, my husband became upset with me. Then, the church leadership started questioning him. Soon after, the emotional affair was exposed. With everything collapsing at once, we began talking about divorce. At that point, we couldn't agree on what this marriage was supposed to look like anymore. And the truth was—I could feel it. He was grieving her. He said she was one of his best friends. And in that moment, I realized something I couldn't unsee I couldn't compete with that. So, I bowed out.

I said, "You know what? I'm not from here. I don't have family here. I've built relationships, but these aren't my people. I'm not staying here like this." So, we continued talking about what divorce would look like for our children.

As we moved forward, my husband said, "We're going to tell the church." In that moment, something in my spirit felt off. My spiritual father even cautioned me, "Don't go to that meeting." But I didn't listen.

There were two meetings scheduled—one for the leaders and one for the entire church. I went to the leaders' meeting. I remember looking at him, and he couldn't even look me in the eyes. That was the moment I knew something was about to happen.

The overseer stood up and said, "These things happen. Life goes on. They're getting a divorce."

The impact was immediate. The leaders didn't know. As they started crying, I walked out. I hadn't signed up for this kind of exposure or humiliation. Sitting in my car, crying uncontrollably, I realized my shock had shifted into shame. It's one thing for a few people to know your business. It's another when everybody does. As a private person, having my life announced publicly was overwhelming.

When I got home, my phone was blowing up. People from our previous ministry were calling, asking, *"Are you okay? What's going on? Where are you going?"*

Meanwhile, in the second meeting—the one for the entire church—they blamed me. They said because of what was happening at home, he couldn't function in his pastoral role. They threw me under the bus. There were about 300 people there, and apparently, it went *sideways.*

His family told me they started defending me. People were yelling. There were arguments, even fights breaking out. All because they knew what was being said wasn't true.

And I wasn't even there. I was at home, watching everything unravel from a distance. I could've fought. I could've gone live. Made a statement. Started my own church. People were ready to follow me. But I didn't. I chose peace. I backed away and said, *"You can have it."*

If you ask anyone from that time, they'll tell you the same thing: I never defended myself publicly. I just walked away. During that season, I had some of the hardest conversations with God I've ever had. Because I knew God had shown me family ministry. And now my family was falling apart. I felt like a failure. My family looked up to me. I had been the "first" in so many areas. My mom would say, "Y'all look like a strong, beautiful couple."

Amid all of this, my sense of strength gave way. I started having panic attacks.

I didn't even know what they were at first. I couldn't breathe. I thought I was dying. The first time it happened, I was in my closet.

I stopped eating, and I lost significant weight. I was exhausted. I remember crying out to God: *"Help me.* I can't do this."

I had two daughters who needed answers. My oldest especially struggled. She couldn't imagine life without us being together. Everyone around her had married parents. To her, it felt like her whole world was falling apart.

Some days, I would sit in my garage before going inside to them—just crying. And the hardest part? I was still helping other families heal…all while mine was breaking. I remember telling God, "I don't deserve this." People were talking—at beauty shops, barbershops, everywhere. Saying things about me that weren't even true. It was humiliating.

And in the middle of all of that, he felt emotionally disconnected. Avoidant. Conversations didn't go well. He had promised to support me financially, but that stopped after a few months. I had to hire a lawyer. Spend thousands of dollars just to make things fair. And even then—it wasn't fair.

I remember telling God: "This isn't right."

Looking back after everything settled, I can see it clearly now: we didn't know each other in every season.

And that matters. I wasn't the partner I thought I was—I was leading. Managing. Carrying things.

He was passive. And the things he praised me for in the beginning, he later resented me for. I wasn't a wife—I was functioning like a parent. And that created resentment on both sides. I was resentful because I felt like I was carrying everything. And maybe he was resentful because I was carrying everything.

I learned something in that season that changed me forever: You have to know what you can submit to. And I didn't have that. I'm a mama's girl. And after everything, I realized—I needed my mom. I had spent so many years away from her, trying to build, become, and hold everything together. But in that season, I just knew…I needed to be where my mom was. That was a hard decision, but it was necessary. So, I went where she was.

When I got there, I still did a little bit of ministry on the side— but very little. And honestly, I thought I was done. I told God, "I think I can retire. I've been doing ministry for almost 20 years. That was a good run. Let me do something different."

But God said, "No." Plain and simple—*no*.

I didn't know what life was going to look like. To be honest, I was tired. I had been hurt in church before, and I didn't have the kind of community I needed. Because of that, I wasn't even sure I wanted a church community anymore. I wanted something different—I wanted a real connection. I wanted to feel safe again. But even in that reflection, God kept gently pulling me back—through opportunities, through people, through moments that reminded me there was still something in me.

I remember one of the first times I shared my story after everything I had gone through. I had gone back to a place where I had preached before, and I was asked to speak at a women's tea. This was the first time I really opened up—not in full detail, but enough to tell the truth. And I remember looking out at a room full of women—tears were everywhere. Healing was happening. And in that moment, I knew: This wasn't just for me. Everything I had gone through—God was going to use it. Because the truth is, I could have lost my mind. But I didn't.

I kept going.

I kept showing up.

I kept pouring into people, even while I was still healing.

I kept counseling, encouraging, speaking—doing the very things God had called me to do. So, I paused from full-time ministry, but I never fully stopped. People continued to invite me to events, fly me out, and ask for my partnership.

Even when I had said, "No"—because I did say no for a season—I knew deep down that it wasn't a permanent answer. It was just a pause. And then IMRSN happened.

Before that, I had found a church where I attended, I tithed—but I didn't serve. I told God, "I'll come. I'll give. But I'm not doing anything else."

I had boundaries. But IMRSN was different. It felt different. I remember thinking, *"God, I've never seen ministry like this. I've never experienced it like this. What are You saying to me?"*

And His voice was clear: "You've rested. Now it's time to be activated."

That's what IMRSN gave me—activation. It reminded me that there was still something in me.

That I wasn't done.

That I wasn't disqualified.

That I had just been on the bench…

But now I was back in the game.

And in that process, I also found something else: Forgiveness. I learned to forgive my ex-husband. That's why I'm not bitter. I pray for him. I genuinely want healing—for him, for me, and for our daughters. I even encourage our daughters, "Let's pray for him. Let's believe in restoring your relationship with your father." Because I'm not angry. And I've learned something powerful: You can go through something traumatic and still choose not to carry bitterness on the other side.

* * *

When I think about it all—everything I've been through…I can finally name it. I went through a rocky childhood and still found the strength to rise above it—to accomplish things my parents didn't have the opportunity to.

I went through church hurt—real church hurt—and still chose not to walk away from God.

I went through betrayal from people who said they loved me… people who were in my life, in my space, but didn't truly have my best interests at heart.

I went through a level of betrayal that could have made me shut down completely…that could have made me never want to love again.

I went through parenting in dark seasons—questioning if I was getting it right, questioning if I had caused damage to my children.

I went through guilt. Shame. Having people know my story but not truly know me.

I went through feeling misunderstood. Feeling unseen. I felt like people were connected to me because of what I carried, not because of who I was.

I went through all of that.

But I also went through forgiveness. The kind of forgiveness that frees you. The kind that says, "I'm letting this go so I can move forward." I went through God repairing my heart. Piece by piece.

I went through the process of reconnecting with people, purpose, and myself.

I went through learning how to forgive people who hurt me… and truly letting them off the hook.

And I went through reparenting myself…giving myself what I didn't receive. Becoming whole in places I didn't even realize were broken.

And now I can say this with confidence: I went through it, but I'm not stuck in it.

I'm healed.

I'm whole.

And I'm still becoming.

* * *

To the one who has spent most of their life being strong for everyone else. The one who watched her mother love a man who kept hurting her made a vow that would never be her story. The one who built walls early and called it wisdom. The one who served faithfully, led quietly, poured herself into other people's healing—and never imagined that one day she would be the one sitting in a parking garage, crying before she could even walk through the door to face her own children.

I went through this for you.

So, you would know that deciding early who you would never become does not protect you from pain. It just changes its shape. I hardened my heart against a certain kind of love because of what I watched my mother endure. I told myself I would never tolerate it. And I didn't—not that kind. But I still ended up in a marriage where I was carrying more than my share, leading when I should have been partnering, and managing when I should have been being loved.

The pain looked different than my mother's. But it was still painful. And learning to name it—without shame, without comparing it to someone else's suffering—was one of the hardest things I have ever done.

I went through this for you.

For the woman who gave everything to a ministry, only to have it taken from her. Who sat in a meeting and heard her life announced to a room full of people without her permission. Who was blamed publicly for things that were not her fault—and had to choose, in real time, whether to fight back or walk away with her dignity. I chose to walk away. Not because I was weak, but because I was clear.

I gave it all away—the platform, the title, the narrative—and I kept my peace. That decision cost me. But it also saved me. And I want you to know that choosing peace over vindication is not losing. It is the hardest kind of winning there is.

I went through this for you.

For the woman who didn't know what a panic attack was until she was standing in her own closet, unable to breathe, wondering if she was dying. For the woman who stopped eating, who dropped weight, who cried out to God in the middle of the night. And not with eloquent prayers, but with the only words she had left: "Help me. I can't do this." I want you to know that God heard every single one of those prayers. Even the ones that weren't finished. Even the ones that were just tears. He was in that closet with you. He is in your closet right now.

I went through this for you.

For the mother who had to hold herself together in front of her daughters while she was falling apart inside. Who sat in the garage and cried before going in, so they wouldn't see the weight of it; who had to answer questions she didn't have answers to yet. Who worried—deeply, quietly—whether the breaking of her marriage would break something in them too. I want you to know that your children are watching something more powerful than a perfect family. They are watching a woman refuse to be destroyed. They are watching someone choose healing over bitterness, prayer over retaliation, wholeness over performance. That is not damage. That is a legacy.

I went through this for you.

For the woman in ministry who thought she was done. Who told God she had given enough, served enough, trusted enough—and maybe it was time to retire from all of it. Who needed a season of just sitting in a pew without being responsible for anyone else; I understand that need completely. Your time of rest was not a failure. The pause was not permanent. God was not finished with you—He was just repairing you. And there is a difference between being benched and being broken. You were on the bench. And when the time came, He put you back in.

I went through this for you.

So, you would know that betrayal—even from someone who called you sister, even from someone whose child carried your name, even from someone you sat beside in worship—does not have the final word over your life. Forgiveness is not a feeling. It is a decision you make over and over again, some days more easily than others. But on the other side of it is a freedom that bitterness could never give you. I pray for him. I genuinely pray for healing over my daughters' relationship with their father. Not because what happened was acceptable—but because I refuse to carry what was never mine to carry in the first place.

I went through this for you.

To the woman who feels misunderstood—seen for what she carries but not for who she is. To the woman who has been hurt by the church and still loves God. To the woman who built someone else's vision and then had to start over with nothing but her own calling and her own voice. To the woman who is still in the middle of her breaking and cannot yet see how God is going to use any of it.

Remember, He is going to use all of it. Every panel you sat on after your life fell apart. Every room you walked into, still standing, when you had every reason not to be. Every tear you cried in private so you could show up in public. Every time you choose your daughters over your grief. Every Sunday, you sat in a pew and received instead of giving—that was not wasted time. That was God rebuilding you from the inside out.

You are not stuck in what you went through.

You are not defined by what was done to you.

You are not disqualified by what fell apart.

You are healed. You are whole. And you are still becoming.

I went through this for you.

With love,

Monique

Chapter 15

Kristina's Transformation

"Choosing Healing"

Immediately after everything happened, I went back to church. I had reached the lowest point of my life. I remember coming home one evening after work, completely drained. I stepped into the shower, and as the water ran, I slid down to the floor. I just sat there crying.

I remember saying out loud, "Okay God, I'm done. I can't do this anymore. Unless You step in, I don't know how I'm going to make it." That moment felt like surrender.

After that, I went back to church. I started serving again. I started showing up. I started doing everything I knew to do. But I also knew something else: I couldn't get through this on my own. Years earlier, I had gone to therapy, and for some reason, that memory came to the forefront of my mind. So, I immediately found a therapist and started going regularly. I knew I needed professional help because everything inside of me felt twisted and confusing.

At the same time, I realized how isolated my life had become. During the relationship, I had slowly distanced myself from almost everyone. I began trying to reconnect with people. I tried to mend friendships that had been damaged and build new ones.

Most new friendships were formed at church and the gym, both naturally social places that made connecting easier when I lacked the emotional energy to initiate. While new friends came easily, repairing old friendships was harder. I often apologized but struggled to explain why, as I hadn't fully processed everything. Some people forgave me; some didn't. I understood both.

Many of those friendships were tied to a life I wanted to move on from. While I wanted to repair them, part of me felt the need to cut off anything linked to that painful chapter. It was complicated.

During that time, two friendships became incredibly important to me. I met both of them at the gym, and they are still close friends today. What made them so impactful wasn't anything dramatic. They weren't demanding friends. They didn't pressure me to talk about things before I was ready. Sometimes we would simply sit together in silence on the couch. Strangely enough, though, that was exactly what I needed. They had an ability to sense when something was off. On days when I was struggling, they would show up, pick me up, and we would get food or go for a walk. Nothing extravagant. Just presence.

Trusting them—and myself as a friend—was hard at first. I hadn't always been a good friend and felt guilty. Their loyalty during my hardest season meant more than they know.

A few months after we met, I finally told them the truth about what had happened. I don't even remember exactly how the conversation started. I just remember feeling safe enough to finally say the words out loud. When I told them, they responded with compassion and love. One of them had experienced something similar in her own life, which created an immediate sense of understanding. For the first time, saying the truth out loud didn't feel like exposing a shameful secret. It felt like releasing something that had been weighing on me.

At the same time, my relationship with God was beginning to shift. Growing up, I had always been around the church. But during the years leading up to that relationship, my faith had become distant and transactional. I thought I had to earn God's trust back.

For a long time, I believed that if I had just made better choices, maybe none of this would have happened. I had to face the reality that while not everything was my fault, many of the consequences I was experiencing came from decisions I had made. That realization was painful, but necessary. I had to relearn how to hear God's voice again.

My life had been so loud for so long—chaos, confusion, constant emotional turbulence—that it felt like God had been absent. But when I looked back honestly, I realized He had been speaking the whole time. There had been moments when I felt that quiet internal warning.

Don't go there.

Don't do that.

But I had ignored it. Part of my healing was learning to recognize His voice again. Learning to trust that voice. I also had to relearn who God actually was.

For a long time, I subconsciously viewed Him the way I viewed the men in my life—as someone who would eventually disappoint me. Someone distant. Someone strict. But slowly, through prayer, therapy, and quiet moments of reflection, my understanding began to change. I started learning how to see Him as a Father. Not just a distant God, but someone who was patient with me, even when I was learning the same lessons over and over again.

As time went on, something else began to change, too: my understanding of myself. Therapy helped me see patterns in my life that

I had never recognized before. I began to understand my triggers, my fears, and the unhealthy coping mechanisms I had developed over the years. For the first time, I was learning who I actually was.

Before that, I had been trying to find my identity in other people through relationships, validation, attention, and approval. I thought those things would tell me who I was. But they never did.

Now I understand that my identity comes from God. That truth changed everything.

Today, I can say something I never would have believed years ago: I know who I am.

Not perfectly. Not without flaws. But I know where I fall short. I know what triggers me. I know what areas I'm still working on. And instead of avoiding those things, I'm learning how to face them in a healthy way.

Before, my instinct was to dissociate, avoid, or suppress pain. Now I know how to process it.

If I were to meet the right man today, I know I would show up differently than I did before. Not because I'm perfect, but because I'm aware. I'm grounded. I know my value, and I know the voice of the God who speaks into my life.

When I think about the title of this book—I Went Through This for You—a few words come to mind.

Identity.

Abuse.

Healing.

Those three words summarize so much of my story. For a long time, I didn't know who I was. I searched for identity in people and relationships that could never give it to me. I experienced abuse that almost convinced me my voice didn't matter. And then I had to walk through the long, slow process of healing.

But if there is one thing I want someone reading my story to know, it is this: You will make it out.

You will find your voice again. And life becomes so much lighter when you stop trying to figure everything out alone and begin walking with God beside you. Because the truth is, the version of you waiting on the other side of healing is stronger than you ever imagined.

* * *

I want to talk to you—the one who learned how to disappear long before anyone taught her that was wrong.

The one who carried a heaviness she had no language for. Who felt alone in a room full of people, out of place in spaces that should have felt like home, and somehow always just slightly outside of belonging. I know what it is to mask almost anything without batting an eye—to read the room, become what it needed, and tuck the real version of yourself so far down that eventually even you forgot where you put her. That hiding made sense once. It kept you safe. But at some point, the very thing that protected you became the wall that kept everyone out, including the people who genuinely wanted in.

I went through this for you.

For the pastor's kid who grew up in church but never felt safe with God. Who performed faith because performance was the only language the environment allowed. Who sat in the front row carrying things that the pew was supposed to be for but couldn't put them down because the expectation was to already have it together. I want you to know that God was never the one demanding that performance. That was people. And there is a version of Him—patient, present, close—that has nothing to do with the version you were handed. He was there in the silence you carried. He is here now.

I went through this for you.

For the woman who ran. Who packed up her life and moved across the country, not because God said go, but because the pain said run—and the two can feel identical when you are hurting enough. I understand that move completely. I understand thinking that if you could just get far enough away from the place where it all happened, the thing itself would stay behind. But pain is not geographical. It lives in the body. It lives in the patterns. It travels with you. And what you find when you land somewhere new is not a clean slate—it is yourself, waiting.

I went through this for you.

For the woman who didn't recognize the danger she was in until her body started telling her what her mind refused to accept. Who stayed not because she was weak but because chaos had become so familiar that peace felt like the thing to be afraid of. I want you to hear this clearly—the confusion was not stupidity. Staying was not foolish. You were surviving a situation that was designed to make you doubt yourself. And the fact that you eventually listened, that you eventually got out, is not a small thing. It is everything.

I went through this for you.

For the woman sitting on the shower floor at her lowest point, saying out loud to God: "I'm done. I can't do this anymore. Unless You step in, I don't know how I'm going to make it." Your prayer was heard. Your moment of surrender—ugly and exhausted and without any eloquence—was one of the most powerful things you have ever done. You didn't have to be composed for God to meet you there. You just had to be honest. And you were.

I went through this for you.

For the woman in therapy learning for the first time that she has patterns—that the things she did to survive made sense once, but are costing her now. Healing is not a moment. It is a slow, necessary, sometimes quiet process of learning who you actually are underneath everything you learned to perform. But on the other side of it is something you may have never experienced before—yourself. Your actual self. The one who was never lost, just buried. And she is worth meeting.

I went through this for you.

So, you would know that identity was never something another person could hand you. The relationship, validation, or approval— none of it was ever going to tell you who you were. What I found, slowly and with a lot of help, is that who I am was never missing. It was just underneath everything I had been carrying.

You are not too broken to be found.

You are not too far gone to heal.

You are not disqualified by what you ran from, what you survived, or what you stayed in too long.

The version of you waiting on the other side of this—the one who knows her triggers, knows her value, knows the voice of God when He speaks—she is already in there. She has been in there the whole time. You will find your voice again.

I went through this for you.

With love,

Kristina

Chapter 16

The Eighth Woman

———————◆———————

"You"

You have made it to the last pages. That is not a small thing. You have sat with seven women through their breaking points and their rebuilding. You have witnessed what it costs to survive the things that were never supposed to happen, and what it looks like when God takes the ruins of a life and builds something from them that no one saw coming. You have read things that were written in vulnerability and offered to you at great personal cost—secrets, confessions, and wounds. These women exercised the very specific kind of courage it takes to say out loud: "This happened to me, and I am going to hand it to you, so you don't have to carry yours alone." And now we have a question for you. *What happened to you?*

＊ ＊ ＊

We are almost arrogantly certain of something. Even if your story does not look exactly like any of ours—even if you have never experienced abandonment or infant loss or abuse or the particular grief of watching a marriage fall apart—we are certain that you can relate in some way. That you have had some of the same questions. That you have stood in a place of deep uncertainty and asked God why, or how, or whether you were going to make it through. That you have experienced Him in the same ways we have described—sometimes clearly, sometimes as a whisper you almost talked yourself out of hearing. And sometimes only in hindsight, looking back at a season that nearly broke you and realizing He was there the entire time.

This book was written for exactly that person. The one who thought her story was too specific, too messy, too ordinary, or too far gone to matter to anyone else. The one who has been carrying something that she has never put into words because she wasn't sure anyone would understand. The one who is still in the middle of it and can't yet see the other side. We see you. And we have a request.

* * *

You are the eighth woman in this book. We did not give you a chapter number. We did not give you a title or a cliffhanger. But you have been here from the very first page. You are the reason why this book exists; you are the person we were writing for before we knew your name. Every story in these pages was shaped by the hope that it would find *you*. Every woman who said "Yes," and told the truth about what she went through did it because she believed that somewhere, someone would eventually hold this book. These are the pages they needed to read, and that someone is *you*.

Now that you have finished reading, we want you to understand something that we believe with everything in us: what you have survived was never only about you. Life is lived forward, but it is understood when you look back. And when you look back—really look, honestly and without flinching—we believe you will begin to see that some of what you went through was preparation. That God was not punishing you or abandoning you or ignoring you. He was equipping you. He was building in you the very thing that someone else is going to need from you. He was writing, through the pages of your pain, a story that belongs not only to you but to the person who is going to need to hear it.

* * *

Scripture says it clearly. 1 Peter 3:15, NIV reads: "But in your hearts revere Christ as Lord. Always be prepared to give an answer to everyone who asks you to give the reason for the hope that you have. But do this with gentleness and respect. "That is what every woman in this book has done. This is our answer—offered with gentleness and respect—to everyone who has ever looked at one of us and wondered how we were still standing. How do we still have hope? How could we go through what we went through and come out with something other than bitterness? This is "our" *how*. This is our *why*. Not because any of us arrived somewhere perfect. But because we decided that the cost of our healing was worth it, and that the story we were given was not meant to end with us.

Remember that Revelation 12:11, NIV states: "They triumphed over him by the blood of the Lamb and by the word of their testimony; they did not love their lives so much as to shrink from death. "Seven women in this book made themselves vulnerable to public opinion, to judgment, to the discomfort of being fully known by strangers, because they decided it was more important to reach a hand back than to protect their image. They did not love their comfort or their reputation so much that they shrank from the exposure of honesty. They spoke their testimony.

And that—the Scripture tells us—is how the enemy is defeated. Not by pretending the battle didn't happen. Not by keeping the story private. But by saying out loud: here is what I went through, and here is what God did in it, and I am telling you because you need to know it is possible. Your testimony has that same power.

Whether you speak it to one person or to thousands, whether you write it in a book or whisper it over coffee to a friend who is barely holding on—it has **power**. It makes an impact. It is seen by God and counted by Him as ministry. He is not a respecter of platforms. He is a respecter of obedience. And He has been asking you to tell your story for longer than you might realize.

* * *

You have heard from us. We told the truth about what our testimony cost, what it built, and what God did in the middle of it. Some of our struggles are far from over. Some of us are still in the process of becoming. Some of us have found deep joy on the other side of seasons we were not sure we would survive. But every single one of us chose to hand you something—something real, something earned, something that belongs to you now. We went through this for you.

And now we have a request: Write your story.

Paint it. Record it. Document it.

Whatever form it takes—whatever your version of handing it to someone else looks like—tell it. Share it. Don't allow it to be only what took place in your life. Let God use it to bless someone else. Let the healing you have received become the very thing that helps another woman find hers. Give yourself the opportunity to reach back—even if it's just for one woman. Even if you never know her name. Even if the only evidence you ever have that your story mattered is the quiet, certain knowledge that you were obedient—that you didn't keep your testimony to yourself. That you gave it away. That you trusted God with the reach. Because someone behind you is standing right where you used to stand. And she needs to know that you made it.

* * *

To every woman who shared her story in these pages—thank you. You opened your life to me personally. You trusted me with the most sacred and difficult parts of your journey. And together we have woven something that is not just a collection of individual stories, but an interwoven cord—seven voices, seven seasons, seven proofs that God does not waste a single thing He allows. That He is faithful in ways we cannot always track in real time.

That the breaking is not the ending.

That rebuilding is possible.

That reaching back is the whole point.

What we went through was not just for us. We chose to use it as a platform. And now, eighth woman—it is *your* turn. Finish your story. And don't forget to reach back.

We went through this for you.

Author Bios

Sylvia Black

Sylvia Black is a 40-year-old wife, mom, stroke survivor, nurse, friend, sister, daughter, prayer warrior, public speaker, heart health advocate, and aunt of two who enjoys the simple things in life. She can save your life if you're choking—and she can make a mean roast! When she's not saving lives through case management nursing care, she's busy doing God's work and sharing her God-given story of faith.

Sylvia is an alumna of Texas Christian University, where she earned her Bachelor of Science in Nursing, and of the University of North Texas Health Science Center, where she earned a Master of Public Health—a degree she uses to shed light on the health disparities that plague vulnerable populations.

Sylvia resides in Charlotte, NC, with her husband and the three beautiful children gifted to her through her covenant marriage: Anyah (21), and fraternal twins Lindan and Weston (12), who have grown her in the best hood—motherhood. Happily married for six years, she and her husband are both ordained ministers and enjoy serving in their local church body. She often volunteers in local health initiatives, educating vulnerable populations on heart health, diabetes, and the social determinants of health. She has an amazing circle of friends and looks to uplift every sister she meets—a heart she pours into her *I Went Through This for You chapter.*

Sylvia is available to book for
speaking engagements, workshops, and events.
For inquiries, contact Sylvia@Throughthisforyou.com.

Renee Hines Blair

Renee is a mother of four, a blended family builder, and a woman who has learned firsthand that love can be both a loss and a gift in the same lifetime. She spent years alongside her late husband, Pastor Corey, serving in church leadership as First Lady—a role she carried with grace, faith, and a devotion to the people they were called to shepherd together.

After his sudden passing, Renee rebuilt her life one intentional step at a time—selling the house, moving forward, welcoming a new son into the world, and eventually opening her heart to love again. Today, she works in residential property management, where her gift for creating community and making people feel at home shines through in everything she does.

Renee is passionate about speaking directly to women who have experienced the specific kind of grief that comes with losing a spouse—the loneliness of it, the complexity of raising children through it, and the quiet courage it takes to let your heart remain open. Her message is simple and hard-won: you will be okay. And one day, without asking permission, you will feel joy again.

To invite Renee to speak at your event, workshop, or gathering, please email Renee@Throughthisforyou.com.
She looks forward to connecting and learning more about how she can contribute to your community.

Chastinie "Chas" Dixon

Chastinie "Chas" Dixon is a minister, leader, and servant at heart, called to reach people beyond the walls of the church. From her early years in youth ministry to her current role helping lead and build within IMRSN Church in the Dallas—Fort Worth area, her journey has been marked by obedience, growth, and real-life encounters with God.

Chas is known for her transparency, her ability to meet people where they are, and her passion for developing others into who God has called them to be. Whether through leadership, writing, or simply walking alongside people in their process, her heart remains the same: to help others heal, grow, and come into a true relationship with Christ.

Her life is a testament that even through struggle, God still calls, equips, and uses those willing to say yes—and her contribution to *I Went Through This for You* is one more "yes" offered to the next woman who needs to hear that her story isn't over.

Chas would love to hear from you at Chas@throughthisforyou.com.

Lauren Freeman

Lauren Freeman is a wife, mother, pastor's wife, and devoted advocate for women who are learning to walk boldly in their faith—even when the road has been anything but straightforward.

She is the wife of Pastor Brandon Freeman, and together they lead IMRSN Church, a growing church plant in the Dallas—Fort Worth area committed to helping people live, love, and lead like Jesus. Lauren is a proud mother of two and a blended mother of four, navigating the beautiful seasons of watching her children grow into the people God designed them to be. Her faith was shaped early by the influence of her grandmother—a devoted woman of prayer who taught her that seeking God in every season was not optional, but the very foundation of a life that holds.

Before stepping fully into ministry, Lauren served as a seventh- and eighth-grade teacher, investing in young people with the same passion she now brings to the church. Recently, she took a leap of faith and left the classroom to serve alongside her husband, bringing her gifts for teaching, storytelling, and community-building into a new and expanding calling.

Lauren carries a deep love for women and a specific passion for what happens when generations come together—when the woman who has survived something reaches back for the one still in the middle of it. She believes testimony is one of the most powerful forces in the kingdom, and that some of the greatest healing in a community happens around a table where stories are told honestly and no one has to pretend.

I Went Through This for You is the expression of everything she believes about women, faith, pain, purpose, and the God who wastes nothing. It is the book she has known for a decade, she was going to write—and the one she is honored to share with you now.

Lauren loves connecting with
audiences and is available for engagements.
Reach out at Lauren@Throughthisforyou.com.

Nakeisha Freeman

Nakeisha Freeman is a devoted woman of faith, servant leader, and dedicated church administrator with a passion for helping others experience the love and faithfulness of God in tangible ways. She faithfully serves in ministry through administrative and benevolence support, playing a vital role in caring for individuals and families during both seasons of celebration and times of need.

With a strong background in organization, communication, and community care, Nakeisha is known for leading with both excellence and compassion. She has a unique gift for creating order, offering guidance, and extending grace—ensuring that every interaction reflects integrity, warmth, and genuine care.

Nakeisha is a proud and loving mother of two sons who deeply values family and the strength of meaningful relationships. She carries that same nurturing spirit into every space she enters, often serving as a source of encouragement and wisdom for those around her.

She holds a Master of Business Administration, which has shaped her professional approach and sharpened her ability to serve effectively in both ministry and administrative leadership. Her combined life experiences and education have equipped her to navigate complex situations with both wisdom and grace. She is also on track to complete her doctorate.

Her journey has been shaped by a commitment to fully trust God, even in uncertain seasons. Through her experiences, she has developed a resilient faith and a desire to help others move from simply believing truth to living out proven faithfulness daily. Nakeisha is honored to contribute to *I Went Through This for You* and prayerfully hopes her words will inspire others to remain anchored in faith, walk confidently in their purpose, and trust God's plan—on and on.

Nakeisha would love to hear from you at Nakeisha@throughthisforyou.com.

Kristina Lizhnyak

Kristina Lizhnyak writes from a place of lived experience, sharing her journey through abuse, healing, and the rediscovery of her voice. What began as a season marked by confusion, fear, and physical turmoil became the turning point that led her to confront the reality of what she was living in—and ultimately to step away.

Her writing is rooted in honesty, exploring the emotional and psychological layers of trauma alongside the slow, sacred work of rebuilding and finding who she truly is. She hopes her story gives others the courage to recognize their own worth and take the first step toward freedom. Her contribution to *I Went Through This for You* is offered to every woman still searching for her voice in the silence.

Kristina welcomes reader correspondence at
Kristina@throughthisforyou.com.

Monique Sharp

Monique Chanise Sharp is a dynamic speaker, pastor, and counselor with a passion for helping individuals heal, grow, and walk in purpose. Born in Kansas City, Kansas, she holds a Bachelor of Arts in Psychology from Rockhurst University, a Master of Arts in Clinical Counseling, and a Master of Divinity with a concentration in Counseling from Trinity International University.

In 2007, Monique answered the call to ministry, and in 2008, she was licensed and ordained by Pastor Corey Brooks at New Beginnings Church of Chicago. Known for her authentic voice and compassionate delivery, Monique speaks truth with clarity, blending biblical wisdom with clinical insight to reach both the heart and the mind.

Her ministry extends beyond the pulpit and across the globe, having served internationally in the Dominican Republic and South Africa. Whether she is speaking to congregations, students, or communities, Monique empowers others to break cycles, overcome emotional wounds, and step boldly into healing and wholeness.

In her professional role as a school counselor, Monique works daily with youth and families, equipping them with tools for emotional regulation, resilience, and personal growth. Her unique ability to integrate faith and mental health makes her voice especially impactful in today's culture.

Above all, Monique is a devoted mother to her two daughters, Bella and Brynn, whom she considers her greatest blessings and inspiration. Her contribution to *I Went Through This for You* reflects the mission she lives by every day: *"Helping the wounded heal and empowering lives to be transformed."*

Monique welcomes speaking invitations and
can be reached for booking inquiries at
Monique@Throughthisforyou.com.